Y0-BQS-048

A Historical Tour of the Holy Land

By

Beryl Ratzer

A Concise History of the Land of Israel
with photographs and illustrations

gefen
publishing house בית הוצאה לאור

Copyright © Beryl Ratzer
Jerusalem 1996/5757

All rights reserved. No part of this publication may be translated,
reproduced, stored in a retrieval system or transmitted, in any form
or by any means, electronic, mechanical, photocopying, recording or
otherwise, without express written permission from the publishers.

Photography: Beryl Ratzer
Typesetting: Marzel A.S. – Jerusalem
Maps: N. Vitkon
Cover Design: M. Franco

ISBN 965-229-166-8
Edition 9 8 7 6 5 4 3 2 1

Gefen Publishing House Ltd.   Gefen Books
POB 36004, Jerusalem   12 New St., Hewlett
91360 Israel   N.Y., U.S.A. 11557
972-2-538-0247   516-295-2805

Printed in Israel

TO THE READER

The inspiration for "A Historical Tour of the Holy Land" and its planned companion, "A Historical Tour of the Bible", came from the many questions asked by the people I have guided over the years. Thank you all.

This volume is not only for those who have visited Israel and want a souvenir which is more than a collection of beautiful photographs. It is also for those interested in, or intrigued by, the long, and often turbulent history of the Holy Land.

As the Bible, both the Hebrew and Christian scriptures, has been used only as a source for historical knowledge, this book is equally suitable for readers of all religions or no religion at all.

History, for me, used to be about forgotten events and dead people. Through archaeological excavations, history has come alive. I can sense the people and events that passed through this piece of land, wedged between Egypt and the Fertile Crescent. Perhaps this book can convey that feeling to you, the reader.

The length of the chapters differs due to the varied amount of written sources for each period and to the fact that, while sometimes this area was a major player on the stage of history, at others it was desolate and unimportant – not even a minor role!

If your appetite is whetted for more, the bibliography is a good place to begin. A visit is even better.

B.R.

My thanks

*to those who inspired me to write and to those who converted
my computer pages into a real book;*

to **Ori Devir***;*

to **Joel Rappel***;*

to **David Baskott***;*

to **Rev. Robert Becerra***;*

to **my family***, who kept me going when I felt that I had bitten
off more than I could chew;*

and finally, to **my husband***, who, in addition to everything
else, also carried my cameras.*

Contents

Chronology of Historical Periods

Sometimes different names have been used for identical or overlapping periods, depending on the historical events they encompass. The following table highlights those parallel periods and their time frames. The dates are those which are generally accepted, but you may well have a reference book with slightly different dates.

4000 – 3150 BCE	**Chalcolithic Age**
3150 – 1200 BCE	**Early, Middle and Late Bronze Ages**
1200 – 586 BCE	**Iron Age, Israelite Period**

	c 955 – 586 BCE	First Temple
	c 1030 – 928 BCE	United Kingdom
	c 928 – 586 BCE	Kingdom of Judah
	c 928 – 723 BCE	Kingdom of Israel

c: Civia (approximate date)
BCE (before common era) and CE are the alternative designations for BC and AD
    in scholarly literature

538 – 333 BCE	**Persian Period**	
	515 BCE – 70 CE	Second Temple
333 – 63 BCE	**Hellenistic Period**	
	166 – 37 BCE	Hasmonean Dynasty
63 BCE – 633 CE	**Roman Period**	
	63 BCE – 333 CE	Roman Pagan
	70 – c 450	Mishna and Talmud
	333 – 633	Byzantine Period
633 – 1099	**Arab Period**	
1099 – 1287	**Crusader Period**	
1287 – 1517	**Mameluke Period**	
1517 – 1917	**Ottoman Period**	
1917 – 1948	**British Mandate**	
	1920 – 1948	U.N. Mandate
1948 –	**State of Israel**	

Distances (as the crow flies):

Metullah to Eilat 420 km./260 miles

Acco to Jordan river 50 km./31 miles

Nathania to 1949 armistice line 16 km./10 miles

Tel Aviv to Jordan river 70 km./44 miles

Ashdod to Jerusalem 57 km./36 miles

Kinneret (sea of Galilee) 212 metres/650 feet below sea level, max.
     Length & width: 20 km x 12 km / 12 miles x 16 miles

Dead Sea 400/1300 feet metres below sea level, max.
     Length & width: 75 km x 17 km / 47 miles x 11 miles

Places on Map – Numerically

1. Metullah Z-A	19. Megiddo Y-C	37. Hebron Y-F
2. Banias Z-A	20. Beit Shean Z-C	38. Gat X-F
3. Dan Z-A	21. Zichron Ya'acov X-C	39. Beit Guvrin/Maresha Y-E
4. Kiriat Shmona Z-A	22. Caesarea X-C	40. Lachish X-F
5. Hatzor Z-A	23. Nathania X-D	41. Ashdod X-E
6. Safed Z-B	24. Nablus/Shechem Y-D	42. Ashkelon X-E
7. Katzerin Z-B	25. Shiloh Z-D	43. Gaza X-F
8. Rosh haNikra Y-A	26. Beth El Y-E	44. Ein Gedi Z-F
9. Acco Y-B	27. Gibeon Y-E	45. Masada Z-F
10. Haifa X-B	28. Latrun Y-E	46. Arad Y-F
11. Beit Shearim Y-B	29. Jaffa/Tel Aviv X-D	47. Be'er Sheva X-G
12. Sephoris/Zippori Y-B	30. Rishon leZion X-E	48. Sedom Z-G
13. Horns of Hittin Y-B	31. Ramla X-E	49. Avdat Y-H
14. Capernaum Z-B	32. Beit Shemesh Y-E	50. Mizpeh Ramon Y-H
15. Tiberias Z-B	33. Jerusalem Y-E	51. Timna Y-K
16. Nazareth Y-B	34. Jericho Z-E	52. Eilat Y-K
17. Atlit X-C	35. Qumran Z-E	
18. Jezre'el Y-C	36. Bethlehem Y-E	

Scale map of Israel and the Golan

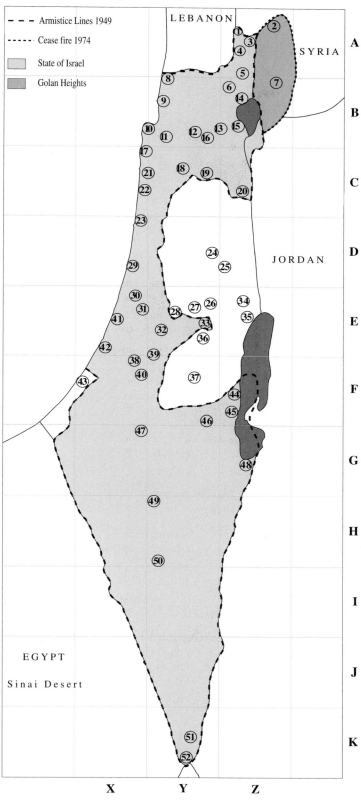

Armistice Lines 1949

Cease fire 1974

State of Israel

Golan Heights

LEBANON

SYRIA

JORDAN

EGYPT

Sinai Desert

Chapter 1   Pre-History to Middle Bronze Age
c1800 BCE

The first chapter of Genesis tells the story of the Creation. Modern scientific studies in physics, geology, cosmology, etc. elaborate, confirm or contest this concise explanation of the beginning of everything.

Travelling the length of the country one can savour the geological splendours and contrasts. Going through the Ramon Machtesh, the strata of the formation of the Earth's crust are exposed in all their beauty. In Timna Park, erosion has created the magnificent pillars, sometimes incorrectly called Solomon's Pillars.

Chemicals in the soil have added colour contrasts, as in the Red Canyon. Earth movement, which causes destructive earthquakes, also created

Sediment layers in the Ramon Machtesh.

waterfalls, such as the chimney near Metulla. The rounded hills of the Golan are extinct volcanoes which spewed out lava – today the black basalt rock.

In the 1930's, in order to build the port of Haifa, extensive quarrying was begun in the Carmel Mountain range. How fortunate that sharp eyes detected the caves of prehistoric man before they were destroyed. Mollusks fossilized into the rocks indicate the changing level of the sea. When pre-historic man used these caves, he could almost cast his fishing line from the cave entrance.

Early man was a nomad, constantly moving, searching for his food – the animals that he hunted. When he realized that not only could he eat some of the things that grow, but could plant and reap and be the master of some of his food requirements, he began the process of settling down.

At the beginning of the century the agronomist Aron Aronson, proved that it was in this area that wild wheat was first domesticated – without even knowing that pre-historic man lived here.

With the process of settling down we enter the Stone Age, so called because man began to use tools – made of stone. The settlements were probably extended family units and, apart from the tools, very little else remains.

About this time there are signs of burial customs. Bodies were sometimes laid in the foetal position and, more important for research, were buried with

Natufian burial in Carmel mountain.

Dolmens in the Golan.

ornaments. These were usually shells or stones and, by analysing the source of these semi-precious stones, one can map the areas covered by trade in those early times.

The burial sites were the earliest stone structures, known as dolmens because of their table-like shape. The Gamla area is dotted with dolmens.

Man's next major stepping stone was when he discovered that some mud, when heated, became hard – the beginning of pottery. The different quality of the pottery, its distinctive shapes and decorations guide the archaeologist in the dating process.

Cave drawing from Mizpeh Ramon museum garden.

Settlements grew beyond the extended family and urbanization began. Settlements were close to a water source, usually sufficiently elevated to give a clear view of the surrounding area, often on one of the main travelling routes. These same locations will be used again and again over the centuries and will become known as tells.

The travelling routes too, were in constant use and form the basis of the modern road system. The Via Maris was the oldest route from Egypt to the north and from there to the Fertile Crescent, traversing the land of Canaan.

Tuthmosis II of Egypt described the route he took to conquer Megiddo about four thousand years ago. Just recently, as the modern road through the same Iron valley was widened, work had to be delayed in order to conduct excavations on ancient sites found along the way.

Jericho boasts of being the oldest city in the world – 8000 years old. How do we define a "city"? Why should people have settled there particularly? For our purposes "city" refers to a settlement where there is building other than huts for living in, when someone has assumed leadership and directed the community to build a wall around their encampment, or a storage pit, or a temple.

Jericho – the oldest city in the Holy Land.

The site which was to become Jericho had two advantages: fresh water from natural springs and its proximity to the lowest point on Earth. The springs ensured abundant food and the lowest place on Earth, the Dead Sea, was the source of salt, without which man cannot survive. Salt was probably one of the first items traded.

About 5,000 years ago man discovered that copper and tin could be mined, heated, alloyed and then used to make tools more efficient than those of stone. Thus was born the Bronze Age.

The archaeological excavations at Timna reveal how pits were dug and furnaces built. An analysis of the slag which was left behind indicates the heat in those furnaces. The temple close by was no less important than the furnace, perhaps more so, for one had to pray for safety and to give thanks to the gods.

For the archaeologist, the temple area provides a wealth of information. The figurines of the gods, the altars, and perhaps even the remains of the sacrifices, help tell a story about ancient man.

Much of our knowledge of this period comes to us from excavations of tells, such as Megiddo, Lachish, Hatzor and Dan. What is a tell?

Israelite gateway at Dan.

Take a small hill, close to a water source. Build a few mud houses on it. Perhaps a wall around them. Burial sites on the slope of the hill. Decades pass. The settlement is deserted – perhaps it was attacked and destroyed, perhaps there was a drought and the people moved. Dust and sand cover everything.

More decades pass. New people build on the ruins. Once again the tell is deserted and rebuilt. Stone buildings instead of mud brick. Thicker walls. A massive gateway. A larger temple area. Again destruction – rebuilding. Dust and sand cover each layer.

This time a different style of gateway. Casemate instead of solid walls. Slowly the little hill grows in height. The final destruction and then it will be covered with dust, dirt and maybe even bushes, or will slowly erode, until a 20th century archaeologist realizes what lies buried in the hill.

Many tells, including those mentioned above, have over twenty identifiable levels. Some, like Arad, are less complicated and have only a few levels.

*Bronze Age gateway
at Megiddo.*

*Narrow passage for use
in times of danger.*

Deciphering the artifacts and buildings found in each level add to our knowledge of the ancient periods.

Positive dating is difficult. Carbon 14 testing has a margin of error of about 200 years and so is only viable when finds are Stone Age and earlier. For later periods, artifacts are correlated with those found in neighbouring areas, such as Egypt, the Fertile Crescent, Asia Minor and the Greek Islands, where there is often an agreed-upon chronology and dating.

The table following should help to connect historical events to archaeological periods.

Date (BCE)	Period	Key historical events and sites
250,000-10,000	Palaeolithic	Early Stone Age, development of man, Carmel caves
10,000-8,000	Mesolithic	Middle Stone Age, settlements
8,000-4,000	Neolithic	New Stone Age, domestication of animals, ceramic pottery, beginning of urbanisation
4,000-3,150	Chalcolithic	Copper and Stone Age, use of copper hieroglyphic script in Egypt, cuneiform in Mesopotamia
3,150-2,200	Early Bronze	Kingdoms of Accad, Sumer, pyramids in Egypt, fortified Canaanite cities, Arad, Hatzor, Megiddo
2,200-1,550	Middle Bronze	Hammurabi, Mari and Ebla archives, Hyksos in Egypt, palaces of Greece and Troy, Patriarchs, Joseph
1,550-1,200	Late Bronze	Egyptian campaigns in Canaan, El Amarna, Ugarit, Mycenia, Israelites slaves in Egypt, Moses

The land of Canaan was not a country with a central ruler. It was made up of many city-states, sometimes allied with one another, sometimes at war, sometimes allied with Egypt, sometimes with the kingdoms of Mesopotamia. It was a land bridge connecting Africa, Europe and Asia, through which the armies of Egypt, of the kingdoms of the Fertile Crescent and the kingdoms of Asia Minor had to pass on their campaigns of military expansion.

Pharaohs and kings listed the Canaanite cities they conquered in the battle annals engraved on their temples. Based on their geographical and topographical descriptions, archaeologists are able to identify such cities as Dan, Hatzor, Lachish, Megiddo and Arad, to name a few.

After the conquest of the land of Canaan by the Israelites, this area became known as the Kingdom of Israel. As we continue from period to period, we will follow the various name changes that occur.

A heiroglyphic inscription from an Egyptian temple.

<table>
<tr><td>Chapter 2</td><td># Hebrew Scriptures
General Introduction</td></tr>
</table>

Chapter 2

Hebrew Scriptures
General Introduction

*T*he Hebrew Scriptures, also known as the Old Testament, are a major source of information for events which took place in the land of Canaan and then in the Kingdoms of Israel and Judah. Inscriptions uncovered in archaeological excavations throughout the ancient Near East are another.

We are going to travel with the Scriptures, dwelling not on the religious, moral or universal message, but wandering along its chronological path, for that is the path this book follows.

In Hebrew, the Scriptures are known as "Tanach" (ta-na-ch), a word made up of three consonants just as the Tanach itself is made up of three separate sections. These are: 1) Torah (ta), The Pentateuch; 2) Nevi-im (na), Prophets; 3) K'tuvim ('ch), The Writings.

The Torah consists of Genesis, Exodus, Leviticus, Numbers and Deuteronomy, traditionally given to Moses on Mt. Sinai. Some Bible critics doubt this, believing that the books

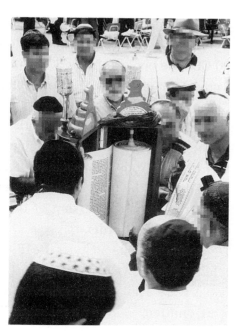

Reading the Torah at the Western Wall. Note the phylacteries on the forehead.

evolved over an extended period. There is no consensus for the disputed dating of any of the five books or their canonization.

Starting with the story of the creation, the Torah continues with the evolution of the descendants of Abraham to become the Israelite people and ends with the death of Moses.

It includes the 613 mitzvot or commandments, which the Israelite nation, and later the Jewish people, are exhorted to obey. It also details the Jewish holy days. One of the fifty three portions into which it is divided is read every shabbat (sabbath).

The books of Joshua, Judges, Samuel I and II and Kings I and II were considered by the sages to have been written by a prophet, so together with Isaiah, Jeremiah, Ezekiel and the 12 minor prophets they make up the section headed "The Prophets".

The canonization of "The Prophets" is generally thought to have taken place circa 200 BCE. Historically, they cover the period from Moses' death to the Babylonian exile after the destruction of the First Temple in 586 BCE.

The last section, K'tuvim, was only finally selected and canonized around 90 CE. The books forming K'tuvim are Psalms, Proverbs, Job, Song of Songs, Ruth, Lamentations, Ecclesiastes, Esther, Daniel, Ezra, Nehemiah and Chronicles I and II.

Ezra and Nehemiah deal with the return of the exiles from Babylon and the beginning of the Second Temple period. Chronicles detail the genealogy and history from Adam to the declaration of Cyrus of Persia allowing the rebuilding of the temple in Jerusalem.

In the Christian version of the Old Testament, these books appear in a slightly different order.

The Apocrypha includes the first and second books of the Maccabees which relate to the Jewish revolt against Greek-Seleucid rule, 165-162 BCE. These books were available when K'tuvim was canonized in the 1st century CE, but were omitted.

The Dead Sea scrolls include the earliest known biblical manuscripts and are generally dated 1st century BCE – 1st century CE. Some are complete, as the Isaiah scroll, some merely fragments. Almost all of these books (each was actually a scroll, written on a long, rolled parchment made of animal hides) were written in Hebrew.

The Tanach, translated into Greek probably sometime in the 3rd century BCE by seventy translators, is known as the Septuagint.

The Vulgate, the Latin translation of the Septuagint by Hieronymus (St. Jerome), was the basis for the best known English version, the King James Bible. Since then, there have been many and varied translations.

Now, let us continue on our journey.

Qumran cave IV where some of the major finds were made.

Chapter 3

Torah – Abraham to Moses
c3800 to c1200 BCE

The biblical stories in Genesis cannot be definitely dated but are usually placed in the archaeological period known as the M.B. (Middle Bronze Age, 1800 to 1600 BCE).

Abraham was born in Ur, at the head of the Persian Gulf. He wandered along the Fertile Crescent to the land known as Canaan, where he settled in the plains around Hebron. His nephew Lot settled in the Jordan Valley, near Sodom, one of the five cities in the fertile plain at the southern end of the Dead Sea.

The biblical narrative tells us that Sodom and its neighbour, Gomorrah, were evil cities and were going to be destroyed by God. Lot managed to flee but was told not to look back. His wife did – and was turned into a pillar of salt.

Archaeological excavations show us that the southern tip of the Dead Sea was fertile, well fed by natural springs and populated. All this was destroyed and the area remained desolate almost up to present times. Today hundreds of thousands of tourists visit there annually.

Thanks to a unique combination of sulphur springs, richly oxygenated air and filtered sun rays (this being the lowest place on earth, 400m or 1300ft below sea level) this area is endowed with therapeutic properties.

Sufferers from psoriasis and other skin diseases, as well as from rheumatic pains, take the cure at the many hotels along the Dead Sea coast. The healthy

Fertile Crescent

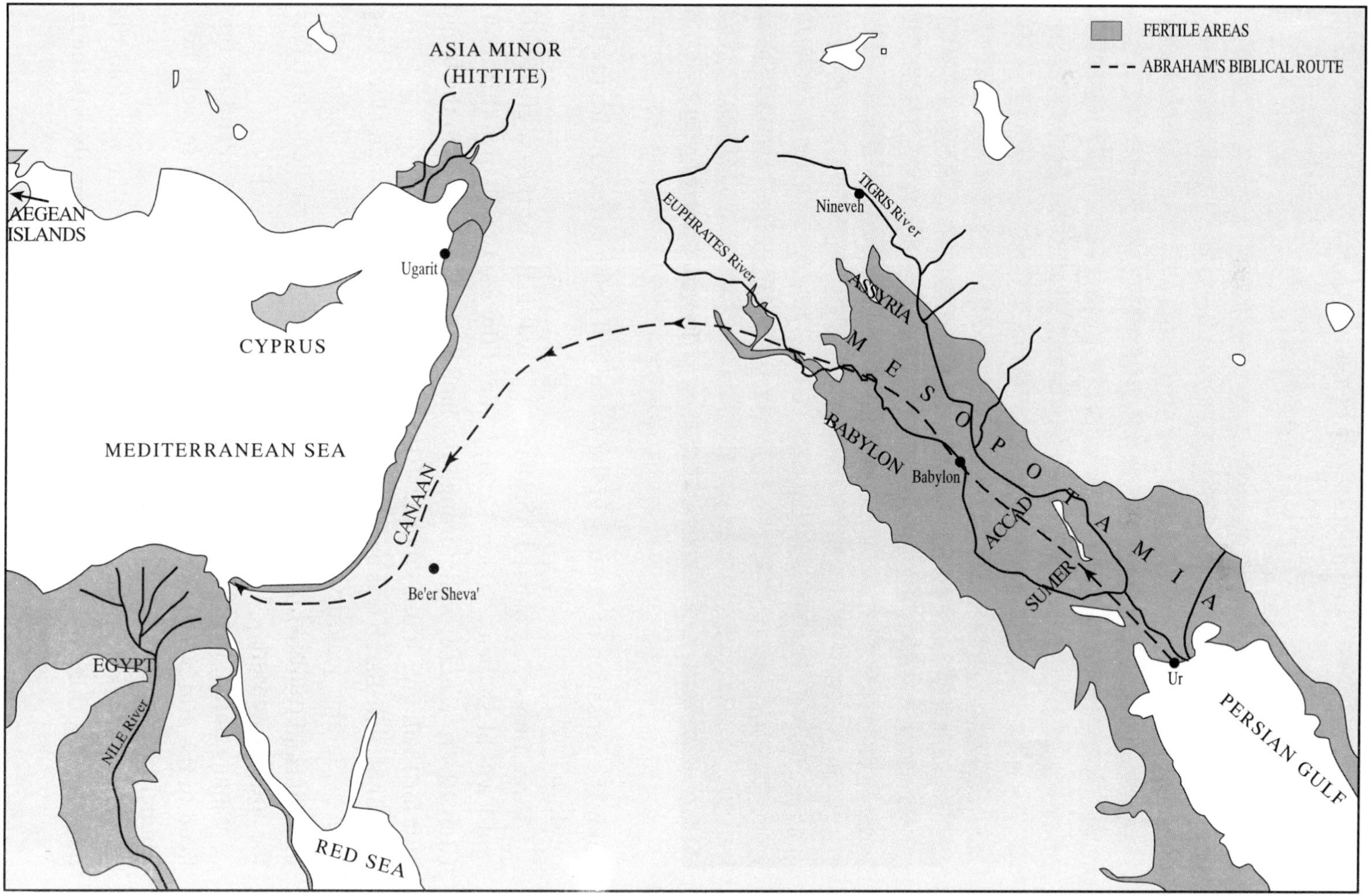

FERTILE AREAS

--- ABRAHAM'S BIBLICAL ROUTE

PERSIAN GULF

Ur

MESOPOTAMIA

SUMER

ACCAD

Babylon

BABYLON

ASSYRIA

Nineveh

TIGRIS River

EUPHRATES River

ASIA MINOR (HITTITE)

Ugarit

CYPRUS

MEDITERRANEAN SEA

CANAAN

Be'er Sheva'

AEGEAN ISLANDS

EGYPT

NILE River

RED SEA

Two mud-covered people.

enjoy the sensation of floating in the water and being covered with the black mud.

Three times God blessed Abraham: "...I will make of thee a great nation and I will bless thee..." (Gen 12:2); "...unto thy seed I will give this land..." (Gen 12:7); "...arise, walk through the land in the length of it, in the breadth of it for I will give it unto thee..." (Gen 13.17)

But his wife Sarah was barren. Ishmael was born of the handmaiden Hagar. Due to Sarah's jealousy they were cast out into the Sinai Desert where, according to tradition, Ishmael became the ancestor of the Bedouin tribes of the southern desert.

Finally Sarah, in her old age, gave birth to Isaac. Abraham and his family lived in the arid Negev in the vicinity of Be'er Sheva', by whose wells he and Abimelech swore a pact of friendship.

Abraham's faith in one God was put to the test when he was told "Take now thy son, thine only son Isaac, whom thou lovest and get thee to the land of Moriah and offer him there as a burnt offering on one of the mountains which I will tell thee of."

Mt. Moriah, where Abraham, ready to sacrifice Isaac, instead sacrificed a ram which was caught in the thicket, is traditionally identified as the place where the First and Second Temples to the God of Israel will be built, and where, today, the Dome of the Rock stands.

When Sarah died, Abraham purchased from Ephron the Hittite a field and cave at Mamre, Cave of the Machpela in Hebron, where he buried her. Here he too was buried, as were his son Isaac and wife Rebecca, their son Jacob and his wife, Leah. (Rachel, another of Jacob's wives, is buried at Bethlehem). Collectively they are known as the Patriarchs and Matriarchs.

Isaac and Rebecca spent most of their life in the arid Negev. Their son Jacob, who cheated his twin brother Esau out of his birthright, fled to Haran, to his mother's brother Laban.

Cave of the Machpela in Hebron.

There he fell in love with Rebecca but was deceived into marrying an older sister Leah. Fourteen years he worked for his uncle Laban, to pay for both wives.

On his return to Canaan he wrestled with the angel, prevailed, and his name was changed to Israel. From this point the story of the patriarchal family widens to become the story of the children of Israel evolving into a nation. The descendants of the twelve sons of Jacob/Israel will become the twelve tribes of Israel.

One of the sons, Joseph, was sold into slavery by his jealous brothers. After many trials and tribulations and successes in deciphering dreams, he rose to the rank of the second most powerful man in Egypt, after the Pharaoh. As such, he was able to offer hospitality to his family, fleeing from famine in the land of Canaan.

On his deathbed, Jacob blessed his own sons and the two sons of Joseph. These blessings are beautifully depicted in the twelve stained glass windows by Marc Chagall in the synagogue of the Hadassah Hospital in Jerusalem.

At this point the book of Genesis comes to an end and the story of the descendants of Jacob/Israel continues in Exodus.

On their arrival, Joseph's family were made welcome in Egypt but over the decades, and perhaps even centuries, their descendants became slaves. Under the leadership of Moses they were led out of Egypt.

There is no agreed dating for the Exodus from Egypt. Most researchers place it in the 13th century BCE. No Pharaoh left for posterity the ignominious detail that during his reign the Israelite slaves departed, so we have no Egyptian sources to help in precise dating.

The location of Mt. Sinai, where Moses received the tablets of the law, has not been positively identified, nor has the route of forty years of wandering in the desert. However, the Ten Commandments, given to Moses, are as valid today as they were then.

The laws in the books of Exodus, Leviticus, Numbers and Deuteronomy are the laws which will guide the children of Israel for the next three thousand years. Broadly speaking, they define man's relationship with God, with man and with nature.

Many laws and customs of the modern world first appeared in the Torah. To cite but a few at random: a day of rest from work on the seventh day; allowing fields to lie fallow (the seventh year); taking care of our sick and our elderly; planting a tree to replace that which we cut down.

The Holy Days, including the Shabbat and the three Pilgrimage Festivals, Pesach (Passover), Shavuot (Weeks) and Succot (Tabernacles) were defined.

Deuteronomy, and the Torah, end with the death of Moses. He blessed the tribes and then went to Mt. Nevo to gaze at the promised land, to which he was denied entry. He died and was buried "but no man knoweth his sepulchre".

Although the use of bronze tools continues while the use of iron spreads gradually, archaeologically the Bronze Age now ends and the next period will be the Iron Age, also known as the Israelite period.

Almost at the summit of Mount Sinai.

Chapter 4	Israelite Period 1200–586 BCE

*O*ur sources for this period, in addition to archaeological excavations, are the books of Joshua, Judges, Samuel, Kings and the various prophets. The major historical divisions are:

1200–1020 BCE	Israelite conquest of Canaan
1020–928 BCE	Saul, David, Solomon
928–721 BCE	Kingdoms of Israel and Judah
721–586 BCE	Kingdom of Judah

Just as there is controversy about the dating of the Exodus, so too is there controversy about the conquest. Was it a rapid process, a slow infiltration, or a mixture of both?

As we have mentioned, the land of Canaan was not a unified country with a central ruler but consisted of many "city-states" each ruled by its own king. At this time, Egypt was in one of her weaker periods and the Canaanite kings were free from foreign domination.

The book of Joshua, as its name implies, relates specifically to Joshua and his deeds. Traditions relating to the tribes in general are preserved in the book of Judges. Both tell of the battles of the conquest. Perhaps there were other sources which have been lost.

Under the leadership of Joshua, the children of Israel crossed the Jordan River. The first city to be conquered was Jericho, whose "walls fell down flat" (Josh 6:20).

Allocations of Israelite Tribes 13th-12th century BCE

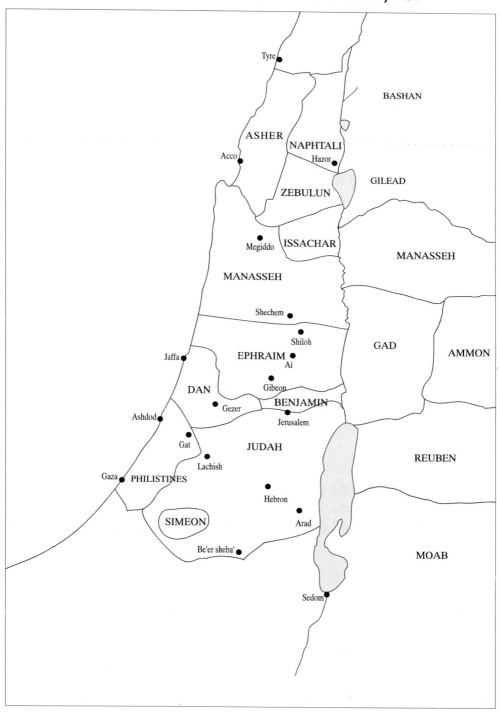

Archaeologists have not as yet identified any walls or remains which can be dated to this period and there are those who cast doubt as to the accuracy of this account of the conquest of Jericho.

Ai, Lachish, Gezer, Hebron, Debir fell to the invading Israelites, completing the conquest in the south. In the north, the kingdoms allied with Hazor were routed.

Joshua called a convocation, erected an altar on Mt. Ebal where sacrifices were offered, and read out to the assembled people the laws given to Moses.

Many of the sites mentioned have been excavated, some identified. The archaeological interpretations of the dating of the walls and buildings and of destruction levels often do not tally with the dating given to the biblical story. Archaeologists debate with one another, as do biblical historians and scholars, sometimes vehemently.

At Shiloh the land was divided amongst the tribes, two and one half tribes on the east bank of the Jordan, nine and one half on the west bank. (Joshua, chapters 13-21)

The description of the Na'hala (inheritance) of each tribe included geographical and topographical details, distances between towns (tells) and their proximity to rivers and mountains. All this taken together helps to identify the many tells dotted about the country. Not always foolproof, but certainly indicative.

The Book of Judges, which covers the period between 1200 BCE and 1040 BCE, starts by listing all the towns not taken by the tribes in their respective areas.

They live among the various Canaanite peoples – Hittites, Amorites, Perizites, Hivites, Jebusites. When they forsook God, "The anger of the Lord was hot against Israel, and he... sold them into the hands of their enemies...". But then "The Lord raised up a judge which delivered them...". (2:14, 16)

This is the message throughout the book of Judges.

The first Judges, Othniel, Ehud ben Gera and Shamgar are only briefly mentioned. The story of Deborah, wife of Lapidoth, is given in greater detail. (Chapters 4 and 5)

Together with her general Barak, Deborah battled against Jabin of Hazor and his captain, Sisera. On the banks of the Kishon river, at the foot of Megiddo, the Canaanite chariots were bogged down in the mud thereby facilitating an Israelite victory. Sisera escaped but was killed by Yael.

The story of Gideon, the next judge, is long and replete with geographical details. At the springs of 'En Harod, Gideon chose an army of three hundred out of the thousands who had volunteered and, using surprise tactics, routed the Midianites. (Chapters 6-8)

One of his seventy sons, Abimelech, mothered by a Canaanite woman, ("for Gideon had many wives") was ambitious. He killed all his brothers (except one, Jotham, who escaped), and set himself up as King of Shechem, which he eventually destroyed. (Chapter 9)

Most archaeologists agree that one of the conflagration levels at Shechem could be dated to this event in the 12th century BCE.

Other judges were Tola, Yair, Yiftach, Ivtzan, Eilon, Abdon and, finally, the last – Samson of Zorah. Many were his escapades. With Delilah of Sorek, Samson finally met his downfall. His hair, source of his strength, was shorn, and he was taken prisoner to Gaza where his eyes were gored out. But the final word was his.

Tied between the two main pillars of the temple in Gaza, he cried "Let me die with the Philistines" as he brought their temple down about his head. (Chapters 13-16)

The book of Samuel covers the years circa 1040 BCE to 970 BCE and starts with the birth of Samuel and his dedication to Eli the priest at Shiloh (which is where the ark of the covenant was kept in a tabernacle).

The Israelites at Eben Ezer were battling the Philistines at Aphek and were losing. The ark brought from Shiloh to protect them was captured by the Philistines who took it to Ashdod.

Fearful that the presence of the ark was responsible for the destruction of the statue of Dagon, the Philistines of Ashdod sent the ark to their compatriots in Gat. When disaster struck there too, it was passed to the Philistines of Ekron (all three were Philistine cities) but the people of Ekron did not want it.

On the advice of their prophets the Philistines placed the ark on a new cart which was hitched to oxen which had never worn a yoke, and then set it free. (I Samuel 5 and 6) The oxen made directly for the Israelite town of Beit

Shemesh. From there the ark was moved to Kiryat Yearim, there to remain until brought to its permanent resting-place in Jerusalem.

The pressure of the Philistines continued and the people appealed to Samuel to "Make us a king to judge us like all nations". Samuel tried to dissuade them but they wanted their king to "Judge us and go out before us and fight our battles". (I Samuel 8)

Samuel annointed Saul whose twenty-year reign was one of war, mainly against the Philistines. Saul would not be the forerunner of a dynasty.

Archaeology has enriched our knowledge of the Philistines. They were one of the Sea People, and the only ones who really left their mark. They reached Canaan in the 12th century BCE, about the same time as the Aegean kingdoms, including Crete, disintegrated. The tomb of Rameses III depicts a sea battle between the Egyptians and the invading Sea People. The event is generally dated 1177 BCE.

The Sea People did not conquer Egypt but settled along the southern coast of Canaan, whether as vassals of Egypt or allies defending her southern border, we cannot be sure. In excavations, a definite Philistine culture can be detected. The Philistines had the knowledge to make iron, as yet unknown to the Israelites. This knowledge gave them a military advantage, as well as better agricultural tools.

The Philistines will eventually be overpowered by David and thereafter play a minor role until their total disappearance by the 8th century BCE.

Between Sochoh and Azeka, separated by the Elah valley, the Israelites and Philistines faced one another. Here it was that David felled Goliath with a river pebble and a sling. (I Samuel 15)

David, and Saul's son, Jonathan, became firm friends. Because of Saul's jealousy, David was forced to flee to the caves of Ein Gedi and eventually took refuge with Achish, one of the Philistine kings.

When the Philistines were once more poised for battle against the Israelites, Achish, unsure of David's loyalty, told David to leave, thereby saving him from the dilemma of what to do if called upon to attack the Israelites.

The Israelites were defeated and Saul's sons were killed. When Saul's body was discovered by the Philistines it was mutilated and displayed on the walls

Burial tomb in the Kidron Valley. At the top, tomb stones in the Mount Olives cemetery.

Beit Shean. The destruction caused by earthquake in the foreground and the reconstructed columns in the rear.

Capernaum. The reconstructed synagogue.

Part of the eastern wall of the Temple Mount which is also the wall of the Old City. In the centre, the Dome of the Rock.

The southwest corner of the Temple Mount showing Robinson's Arch and part of the southern excavations.

The Cardo - the main street in Byzantine Jerusalem.

The Hurva, one of the many synagogues in the Old City destroyed by the Jordanian Legion in 1948.

Church of the Annunciation in Nazareth.

Peter Gallicantu Church in Jerusalem.

The Church of All Nations and the Church of Mary Magdelene on the slope of Mount Olives

Sidonian Tomb at Maresha/Beit Guvrin. The Sidonians were merceneries who settled in the area during the Hellenistic period.

The St. George Monastery in Wadi Kelt. Built into the mountains of the Judean hills by 6th century hermits.

A well camouflaged gazelle at Ein Gedi, an oasis in the Judean desert.

Courtyard of the Pater Noster Church on Mt. Olives where the Lord's Prayer is displayed in over seventy languages.

of Beit Shean. The men of Jabesh Gilead retrieved his body and gave him and his sons a decent burial. (I Samuel 31)

David's magnificent lamentation for Saul and Jonathan ends one period, the reign of Saul, and opens the next, the reign of David.

"The men of Judah came and they annointed David king over Judah...", (II Samuel 2:4) and for the first seven and a half years he ruled from Hebron.

With the conquest of Jebus, captured when Yoav ben Zuriah "getteth up the gutter", (II Samuel 5:8) (perhaps a hint that he gained control of the water supply of the city, causing the people to surrender) the capital now became Jerusalem, city of David.

The final chapter of the book of Samuel tells of David's defiance in taking a population census. To lift the plague that this caused, David was told to purchase the threshing ground of Arouna and there to build an altar and make a sacrifice to God.

In the background, the tell of Beit Shean, on whose walls Saul's head was displayed. In the foreground, the stage of the Roman theatre with settings for a modern performance.

Arouna offered the land as a gift but David insisted on paying a fair price. II Samuel 24:24 and I Chronicles 21:24 record the deed of sale for the piece of land on which David built an altar, and his son Solomon built a Temple. (Traditionally, this is the same spot that Abraham prepared an altar to sacrifice Isaac.)

The Temple built by Solomon will stand over four hundred years, will be destroyed by the Babylonians but very shortly will be rebuilt. The Second Temple, in use for over five hundred years, will be destroyed by the Romans in 70 CE.

View of Jerusalem from the Haas Promenade. In the foreground is the outline of the City of David. To the right the Kidron Valley. In the centre the Southern Wall of the Old City, built by Suliman II in 1517. Above it is the Dome of the Rock, which is on Mt. Moriah, site of the First and Second Temples.

City of David –
archaeological remains
of a house and terrace.

During David's rule the kingdom was strengthened and enlarged. As he lay dying, the fight for the succession began. Adonijah appeared to have taken over the reins but Nathan the Prophet and Bath Sheba reminded David of his promise that Solomon would reign after his death. David instructed Zadok the priest to anoint Solomon at the Gihon spring.

So ends David's rule, which is generally dated circa 1000 BCE to 961 BCE.

Solomon's first act was to consolidate the kingdom. Then, using the iron and cedar, gold and silver prepared by David, Solomon spent seven years building the Temple. He was advised by Hiram the Phoenician, a master builder. The Temple is described in great detail but no archaeological remains have been uncovered.

We are told that Solomon fortified Hazor, Megiddo and Gezer. Professor Yigal Yadin, excavator of Hazor, describes the discovery of what he believed to be Solomon's gates:

"To impress our laborers, even before the contours and plan of the gate become clear, we traced the plan of the Megiddo gates [already excavated – B.R.] on the ground, marking it with pegs to denote corners and walls and then instructed them to dig according to the marking, promising 'here you will find a wall' or 'there you will find a chamber'".

"When our prophecies proved correct our prestige went up enormously... when we read the biblical verse about Solomon's activities in Hazor, Megiddo and Gezer, our prestige took a dive but that of the Scriptures rose sky-high!".

Solomon and the Queen of Sheba exchanged gifts and opened up a trade route to the east coast of Africa via the port of Ezion Geber – Eilat of today. Ethiopian tradition holds that Menelik, the founder of the Ethiopian dynasty, was the son the Queen of Sheba bore to Solomon. The Emperors of Ethiopia, up until Haile Selassie in the 20th century CE, were known as "Lion of Judah", among their other titles.

Solomon was a wise king with a weakness for women – 700 wives and 300 concubines. Many of the marriages were out of political expedience, to cement alliances with Moab, Ammon, Edom, Zidon and the Hittites. The freedom he granted to worship pagan gods angered God. Solomon's descendants would not rule the northern tribes of Israel (I Kings 11:11-13).

In fact the seeds for the division of the kingdom were sown during Solomon's reign. Jeroboam, son of Nebat, had been appointed the overseer of the royal building projects. As his power grew, so too did his appetite.

He was encouraged by the prophet Ahijah of Shiloh, who assured him that God had promised that the descendants of Solomon would not rule the ten tribes of Israel, but that he Jeroboam would.

When Solomon learnt of this plot, Jeroboam was forced to flee to Egypt, where he was offered shelter by Shishak.

Upon Solomon's death, his son, Rehoboam, went to Shechem, to be proclaimed king. The northern tribes sent representatives to voice their grievances. Instead of following the advice given to him by the elders who had served Solomon, Rehoboam threatened to be even more demanding than his father.

Angered, the people of Israel called upon Jeroboam to be their king. Thus, the kingdom created by David and consolidated by Solomon ceased to exist. The separate kingdoms of Judah and Israel came into being.

The beginning of the reigns of Rehoboam and Jeroboam is generally accepted as 922 BCE. The northern kingdom of Israel will exist for two hundred years; the kingdom of Judah for three hundred and thirty six. During those periods, Israel had nineteen kings; Judah had nineteen kings and one queen.

The following table shows when each ruled and who the neighbouring ruler was. Because the Scriptures were not meant to be a history book, there are no definite dates to indicate the beginning or the end of a rule. Setting dates is a matter of analysis, comparisons and deductions. Biblical scholars are not always in agreement so do not be alarmed if you have a book which gives slightly different dates.

Kings of Judah	Kings of Israel	Prophets
928-911 Rehoboam	928-907 Jeroboam	
911-908 Abijam	907-906 Nadav	
908-867 Asa	906-883 Baasha	
	883-882 Elah	
	882-882 Zimri	
	882-871 Omri	
867-846 Jehoshaphat	871-852 Ahab	Elijah
	852-851 Ahaziah	
846-843 Jehoram	851-842 Jehoram	
843-842 Ahaziah		
842-836 Athalia	842-814 Jehu	
	814-800 Jehoahaz	
836-798 Joash	800-784 Jehoash	
798-769 Amaziah	784-748 Jeroboam II	Amos (c760-?)
769-733 Uzziah	748-748 Zecharia	Josea (c740-20)
	748-748 Shallum	
758-743 Jotham	747-737 Menachem	
	737-735 Pehahiah	
	735-733 Pekah	
733-727 Ahaz	733-724 Hoshea	
727-698 Hezekiah		Isaiah (c710-?)
698-642 Menasheh		Nahum (c650)
641-640 Amon		Zephania, Micah, Jonah
640-609 Josiah		Jeremiah (c626-586)
609-609 Jehoahaz		
609-598 Jehoiakim		Habakkuk
597-597 Jehoiachim		
596-586 Zedekiah		Ezekiel (c600-580)

Solomon's Kingdom

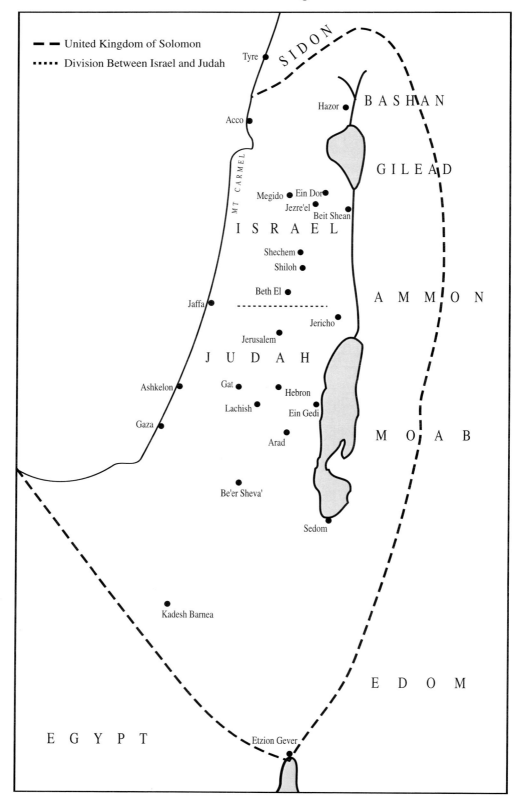

- – – United Kingdom of Solomon
- ···· Division Between Israel and Judah

SIDON

Tyre

BASHAN

Hazor

Acco

GILEAD

MT CARMEL

Megido Ein Dor
Jezre'el
Beit Shean

ISRAEL

Shechem
Shiloh

AMMON

Beth El

Jaffa

Jericho

Jerusalem

JUDAH

Gat
Ashkelon Hebron
Lachish
Ein Gedi

Gaza

Arad

MOAB

Be'er Sheva'

Sedom

Kadesh Barnea

EDOM

EGYPT

Etzion Gever

The size of the two kingdoms depended on the varying strength of the kings of Judah and Israel and of their neighbours.

Judah was the more stable. All the kings were of the Davidian dynasty, Jerusalem was the capital and the Temple was the centre of religious life. However, Judah was the smaller and poorer of the two.

Israel comprised the area of the ten tribes, including the eastern side of the Jordan River. Control of the coastal area meant trade and the fertile land meant abundant agriculture. Changing dynasties meant political unrest.

The books of Kings and Chronicles relate the deeds of all the kings. We will refer to but a few. Inscriptions in the temples and palaces of the Egyptian pharaohs and Fertile Crescent kings often fill in missing historical details.

From an inscription, which included a list of place-names, found on a temple wall in Luxor, and a stele found at Megiddo, we know that Shishak attacked the newly established kingdoms of Israel and Judah.

Jeroboam had the foresight to realise that, unless the people had a place other than the Temple in Jerusalem to offer sacrifices to God, he would lose their loyalty. At two ancient sanctuaries, Dan in the north and Bethel in the south, he placed a golden calf and decreed these to be the sites for offering sacrifices. He also appointed priests who were not of the tribe of Levi and set a new date for the festival of Succot (Tabernacles) thereby finalising the break with Judah.

His capital moved from Shechem to Penuel, in the Gilead, and then to Tirza. His dynasty ended with the murder of his son, Nadav, by Baasha.

After many years of civil war and unrest, Omri and Asa ended the warfare between the two kingdoms. The stele of Mesha of Moab confirms that Omri was a powerful king. He established a new capital at Shomron (Samaria), where he was buried.

To strengthen his ties with the seafaring Phoenicians, Ahab, heir to Omri, married Jezebel daughter of the king of Sidon. She was instrumental in spreading the cults of Baal and Ashtoreth causing the prophet Elijah to proclaim: "As the Lord God of Israel liveth... there shall not be dew nor rain these years, but according to my word". With that he fled to Cherith, where he was fed by ravens. (I Kings 17:1-6)

In the third year of the drought he returned to Israel and, brought before Ahab, demanded that the pagan prophets be assembled on Mount Carmel. There he challenged them to what was in reality a confrontation between monotheism and paganism. Who would send fire to consume the sacrifice, the pagan gods or the Lord?

Elijah taunted the pagan prophets as Baal failed to consume the sacrifice (perhaps he is on a journey, or sleepeth and must be awakened), and as evening fell he prepared his altar and called: "Hear me, oh Lord, that these people might know that thou art the Lord God." (I Kings 18:19-40)

With that, the sacrifice was consumed. Elijah ordered the remorseful people to kill all the false prophets and told Ahab that the drought was ended. However, he fled to Mt. Horev, (also known as Mt. Sinai) to avoid Jezebel's wrath.

Instructed by God to return, he met Elisha and, by casting his mantle over him, indicated that he was to be his successor.

When Jezebel organised two false witnesses so that Ahab could acquire the vineyards of Navot, which he coveted, Elijah informed him that his dynasty would end with his son's short rule.

From an Assyrian obelisk showing Jehu kneeling at the feet of Shalmaneser we learn of the Assyrian subjugation of Israel.

Under Jeroboam II of Israel and Uzziah of Judah a period of peace, prosperity and renewed power lasted about forty years. The prophets Amos and Hosea protested the exploitation by the wealthy classes in Israel.

Judah expanded, reaching as far south as Sinai. For his arrogance Uzziah was afflicted with leprosy and was buried outside the royal tomb. The inscribed tombstone originally placed over his grave was found on the Mt. of Olives.

The rise of Tiglat Pileser (Pul in the scriptures) brought once again the almost total subjugation of Israel by Assyria. The destruction wrought by this invasion can be seen in the excavations at Hatzor and Megiddo.

Israel was reduced by Samaria, besieged by Shalmaneser, and in 723 BCE was finally totally vanquished. From an inscription left by Sargon, we learn that most of the population were exiled to other parts of the Assyrian Empire.

The descendants of these deportees would come to be known as the ten lost tribes of Israel.

As was customary, Assyrian mercenaries and deportees from other conquered areas were moved to Samaria. Together with the Israelites who had not been deported, these would be known as Samaritans.

Judah was temporarily spared the Assyrian assault and Hezekiah set about fortifying his kingdom. In Jerusalem, a tunnel increased the water supply to the city thereby allowing its expansion, as far as the broad wall in the west.

Taking advantage of a Babylonian revolt against Assyria and against Isaiah's advice, Hezekiah stopped paying tribute to Assyria and organised a coalition against her, together with Egypt.

On the walls of Sennacherib's palace in Nineveh is a list of the towns and villages of Judah which were destroyed by the Assyrians, as well as a relief

The Broad Wall, in the Jewish Quarter of the Old City, is from the time of Hezekiah. Its discovery was important as it was the first positive indication that biblical Jerusalem expanded well beyond the confines of the city of David.

First Temple burial tombs on Mt. Scopus.

depicting the storming of Lachish. Jerusalem was under siege but, as prophesied by Isaiah (II Kings 19:7), the Assyrian army departed and Jerusalem was spared from vassalage.

For the next half decade, under Menashe and Amon, all Hezekiah's religious reforms were forgotten and paganism was rife in Judah. Comprehensive reforms were once more introduced by Josiah, to whom some biblical scholars attribute Deuteronomy.

Babylon and Egypt gained independence from a now weakened Assyria. Josiah tried to block the advance of Egypt towards Assyria and was killed at Megiddo. Judah became a vassal of Egypt, but not for long. The campaigns between Egypt and Babylon continued, each trying to inherit the position of dominance vacated by Assyria.

In 598 BCE Jehoiachim and thousands of his subjects were taken as prisoners by Nebuchadnezzer to Babylon. Under the puppet king Zedekiah, and against the advice of Jeremiah, Judah joined Egypt in a revolt against Babylon.

Retribution wasn't long in coming. Judah was laid waste and Jerusalem was completely destroyed. Once more there were deportations to Babylon. Independent Jewish life in the Holy Land, which was laid waste, virtually came to an end. Paradoxically, it would thrive in Babylon.

Chapter 5	# Second Temple Period c538–70 BCE

Introduction

As the heading implies, this chapter covers the entire period during which the Second Temple stood. Using the more common historical or archaeological terms, this chapter has been subdivided according to the powers which ruled the area.

The Babylonian Empire was superseded by the Persian Empire, which was replaced by the Greek Empire, which in turn was conquered by the Roman Empire. Each of these powers left its imprint. In spite of their seeming invincibility, each one exited from the stage of history, never to return again.

The thread which connects all the periods, and continues up until the present moment, is the descendants of those people who built and revered and prayed in that same Temple, and continued to mourn for it after it was destroyed – the Jewish people.

Part of a Hebrew inscription found in the excavation at the south western corner of the Temple Mount, possibly a remnant of the destruction of Jerusalem by the Romans in the year 70.

Persian Period   538–333 BCE

From the books of Jeremiah (32ff) and II Kings (24-5) and from excavations, we learn that the devastation of Judah was widespread. When Gedaliah, who had been appointed governor by the Babylonians, was murdered, many of those who had not been exiled, fled. The Babylonians did not bring in other people (as did the Assyrians when the kingdom of Israel was destroyed) so the population of Judah decreased and consisted of "Vine-growers and husbandmen".(II Kings 25:12)

Cyrus, (who is viewed by Isaiah as "The Lord's anointed") founded the Persian Empire and in 538 BCE, conquered Babylon. The exiles were given permission to return to Jerusalem and rebuild their Temple (Ezra 1:2-3). The prophets Hagai and Zechariah encouraged Sheshbazzar and Zerubabel, who led the returning exiles.

*The Kotel, part of the western supporting wall of the
Herodian Temple Mount enclosure.*

Written sources for this period are scanty but c. 458 BCE Ezra called a convocation of the people at which they renewed their covenant with God. Due to the opposition of the people of Samaria, Ezra was unable to complete the walls of Jerusalem. This was accomplished by Nehemiah.

Papyri, found in Elephantine (Leontis) in Egypt and Wadi Dalya in the Jordan Valley, add to our very meagre knowledge of this period. Coins and jug handles imprinted with "Yahud" (Judah) confirm that Judaea was an autonomous province of the Persian Empire.

The population of the land was varied. Edomites lived in the Negev and as far north as Hebron; the seafaring Phoenicians lived along the northern coast; the Samaritans occupied what had been the kingdom of Israel. In Judaea were the Judaeans, later to be called Jews, with pockets of Sidonians in such places as Maresha.

It is towards the end of this period that the Samaritans made their final break from Judaism. They no longer performed their religious worship or offered sacrifices at the temple in Jerusalem. Instead they built a temple at Mt. Gerizim and appointed their own high priest. They continued to use the Torah but rejected the Oral Law.

This period came to an end with the rise of Alexander of Macedon, under whose leadership the Persian Empire was conquered.

Hellenistic Period 333–63 BCE

As we have seen, historical events in the land of Israel were intrinsically woven into the changes that took place in the Fertile Crescent and Egypt. At this point in history the seat of power shifted westwards to the Mediterranean basin, to the Greek Empire.

The army of Alexander the Great conquered Judah in 332 BCE and swept eastward as far as India. In its wake a new culture took hold – Hellenism.

The untimely death of Alexander, before he was able to consolidate his empire, resulted in its division into three sections – Greece and the Islands, Egypt (ruled by Ptolemy) and Syria (ruled by the Seleucids).

Judaea, after initially being tossed between the Ptolemies and Seleucids in 301 BCE, fell to the Ptolemies and, for the next hundred years, was ruled from Egypt.

Independent administration was introduced with a localised tax system. Greek architecture and town planning led to the spread of new cities-polis. Agriculture flourished and oil, balsam and asphalt were in great demand as exports. Mercenaries and colonists swelled the local population with pagan settlers and temples.

Under the Ptolemies the Jewish population enjoyed religious freedom but this came to an end in 201 BCE. At the Battle of Paneum (Banias) the Seleucids gained control of the area, now to be known as Coele-Syria and Phoenicia.

Jerusalem, although not a polis, continued to be capital of Judaea, an autonomous area governed by the high priest and the council of Elders.

Antiochus Epiphanes (175-164 BCE), needing the revenue provided by polis taxes and temple treasuries, decided to accelerate the Hellenisation process. Jerusalem was made a polis, and named Antiochia. The usual institutions, including a gymnasium next to the temple, were built. A new high priest was appointed, subservient to Antiochus, and not of the line of Zadok.

During an unsuccessful Seleucid invasion of Egypt, partly due to the interference of Rome, there were revolts in Judaea, including in Jerusalem, against the Seleucids. The deposed high priest, Jason, was reinstated.

Antiochus retaliated by taking complete control of Jerusalem. The temple was dedicated to Zeus and strategically overlooking the temple, the citadel, Acra, was built.

Circumcision and sabbath observance were banned, thereby threatening the practice of the Jewish religion. As the Jewish population was forced to participate in the pagan rites at the temple, many Jews left Jerusalem.

Despite the fact that many of the priests in Jerusalem were Hellenists, having been appointed by Antiochus, the general population remained faithful to their religion. They rallied to the banner of Mattathias, a priest living in Modi'in, who called on the people to defy the ban against Jewish observances.

Lead by Judah the Maccabee, (166-160 BCE), son of Mattathias, the rebels won a number of significant battles against the Seleucid forces. In 164 BCE they regained control of Jerusalem and rededicated the temple, even though a Seleucid force held out in the Acra.

The Jewish holiday, Hanukkah (Festival of Lights) commemorates this rededication of the temple. The events leading up to the revolt and the early years of the Hasmonean dynasty are preserved in the books of the Maccabees.

Initially, the rebels suffered some setbacks and temporarily lost Jerusalem, but under Jonathan (160-143 BCE), brother of, and successor to Judah, more areas came under Hasmonean rule.

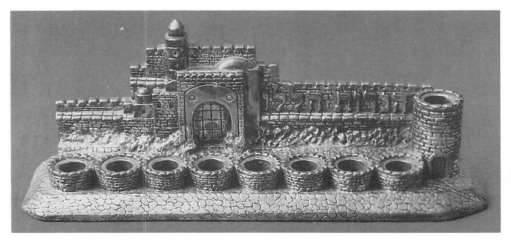

Hannukiah – used during the eight days of the Festival of Lights.

Conquests of Hasmonean Dynasty 166-76 BCE

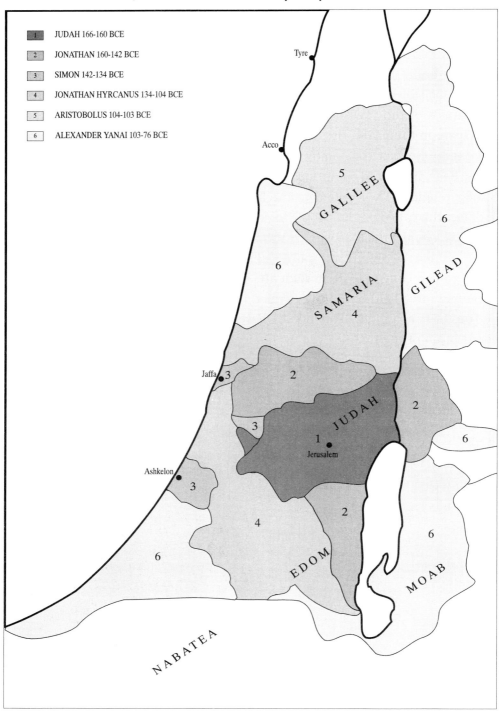

JUDAH 166-160 BCE

JONATHAN 160-142 BCE

SIMON 142-134 BCE

JONATHAN HYRCANUS 134-104 BCE

ARISTOBOLUS 104-103 BCE

ALEXANDER YANAI 103-76 BCE

Diplomacy and politics were as important as victory in battle. Under Judah, a treaty had been signed with Rome, thereby recognizing Judaea as an independent power. Jonathan played off Demetrius I and Alexander Balas, rival aspirants, for control of the Seleucid kingdom, and so gained more territory as well as the position of high priest.

These intrigues eventually cost him his life as he was murdered by Tryphon, to whom he had switched his allegiance, but not before he had established relations with Sparta.

His brother Simon (143-134 BCE), continued to expand the independent areas of Judaea. Exemption from paying tribute to the royal treasury and the privilege of minting his own coins, indicates to us the degree of independence enjoyed by the Hasmonean kingdom of Judah.

In 140 BCE the great assembly in Jerusalem conferred on Simon the titles "ethnarch, high priest and supreme commander of the Judaean nation" and declared these positions hereditary "until a true prophet shall arise" (I Maccabees 14:27ff).

The conquest of Jaffa and Gezer gave access to the sea and the conquest of the Acra restored Jerusalem entirely to Hasmonean rule. Simon (together with two of his sons) was assassinated by his son-in-law.

His third son, John Hyrcanus 134-104 BCE, also exploited the Seleucid-Ptolemian rivalry and expanded even further, absorbing Idumea (Edom) and areas across the Jordan. He also destroyed the Samaritan temple on Mt. Gerizim.

During the rule of Alexander Yannai, 103-76 BCE, whose title was king, the territory of Judaea reached its peak and included control of the Nabataeans. However, for the first time, there was conflict within the Hasmonean kingdom.

The Sadducees (Zedukim, priestly caste) served in the temple. They had been the vanguard of the Hasmonean revolt but in the intervening years had lost their influence over the people, had become the aristocratic rich upper class and were often corrupt.

The Pharisees (Perushim, those who leave or those who interpret) were the sages, the proponents of the oral law. The people respected them and their leadership.

Alexander's support of the Sadducees resulted in a revolt of the Pharisees which was cruelly suppressed. Too late he understood his misjudgement and on his deathbed he urged his wife, Shlomzion Alexandra (76-67 BCE) to compromise with the Pharisees.

During her peaceful rule the Pharisees increased their influence.

Upon her death, her son Aristobolus II (67-63 BCE) ousted his older brother, Hyrcanus II (63-40 BCE), thereby hastening the end of the rule of the Hasmonean dynasty.

Hyrcanus was assisted by Antipater the Idumean and Aretas the Nabataean. At first, Rome intervened in favour of Aristobolus. Pompey conquered Syria, made it a Roman province and then switched his support to Hyrcanus.

Judaea was confined to the areas of Judah, southern Samaria, the Galilee and those parts on the other side of the Jordan with a large Jewish population (Peraea) and had to pay tribute to Rome. Hyrcanus was reduced from king to ethnarch but remained high priest.

And so the Roman period is ushered in.

Hasmonean and Herodian Dynasties

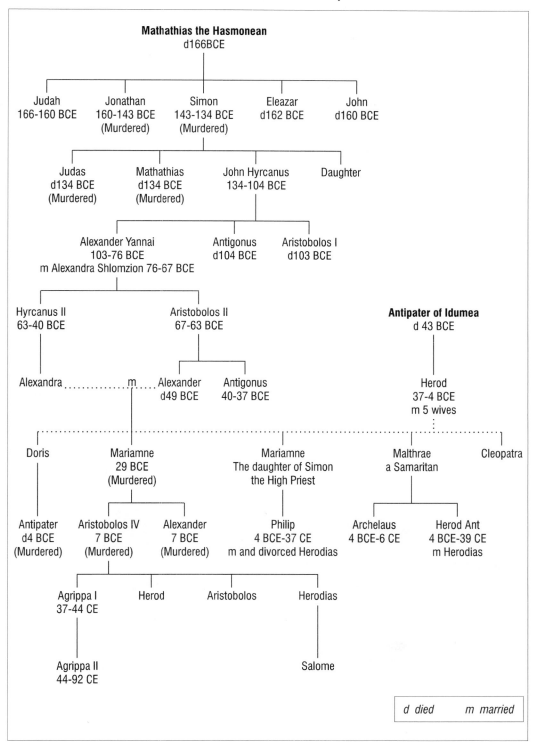

Roman Period   63 BCE – 633 CE
General Introduction

This period can be subdivided into three periods:

The first is 63 BCE to 70 CE. The Second Temple was under Jewish control and at times Rome allowed the transfer of a Temple tax paid by Jews throughout the Empire to be transferred to Jerusalem. The population of Judaea, Galilee and neighbouring areas enjoyed a fluctuating amount of autonomy, ranging from an independant vassal kingdom to direct rule by Roman governors. The Roman Empire was pagan.

The second period is from 70 CE to 333 CE. Rome continued to be pagan. With the destruction of the Temple and the conquest of Galilee and Judaea, the Jews lost most of their independence. During this period the Mishnah and Jerusalem Talmud (Oral Law) were redacted.

The final period is from 333 CE to 633 CE. Christianity became the official religion in what remained of the Roman Empire, part of which had been conquered by the Visigoths, Vandals and barbarians. The Holy Land is ruled by the eastern Byzantine Empire. During this period the Babylonian Talmud was redacted.

Roman theatre at Caesarea.

Roman Period   63 BCE – 70 CE

As we saw in the last chapter, with the ascent of Pompey in Rome and the Roman takeover of Judaea, the size of Judaea was reduced as was the status of Hyrcanus. However, both Hyrcanus and Antipater joined Julius Caesar's camp and when Caesar defeated Pompey in 48 BCE, Caesar was generous to both.

Hyrcanus was reinstated as hereditary ethnarch and Antipater's son, Herod, was appointed governor of Galilee.

Caesar's assassination (44 BCE) did not cause any major upheaval in Judaea until the Parthian invasion (40 BCE). Antigonus, son of Hyrcanus's brother and ex-rival, Aristobolus, allied with the Parthians in an attempt to regain the throne, which he considered to be rightly his.

With the people's support Hyrcanus was imprisoned and his ally, Herod, was forced to flee to Rome to seek military aid. Antigonus was crowned King of Judaea by the people.

In Rome, Anthony and Octavian concluded that Herod was the only one they could trust in Judaea and bestowed on him the title of king. The Roman army succeeded in turning the tide and the Parthians were pushed back, leaving Antigonus without military support.

Aquaduct at Caesarea.

*Roman theatre at
Beit Shean.*

Herod returned to Judaea and with Roman assistance gained control of Idumea, Samaria and the Galilee. When the Parthians were finally defeated, the Roman legions were available to enable Herod to take all of Judah, including Jerusalem. In 37 BCE Antigonus was executed, thereby ending the Hasmonean dynasty.

Herod was completely loyal to Rome, first to Anthony, who had presented the area of Jericho and the lucrative balsam groves to Cleopatra, and then to Augustus. His subjugation of the Nabataeans proved his value to the Romans and the area under his control was increased to include Gaulanitis, Batanaea and Trachonitis in the north-east.

While the Jews of the diaspora benefited from his personal relations with the Roman aristocracy from Augustus down, his own subjects did not. Only the fear that a revolt would diminish his prestige in the eyes of the Romans limited his cruelty, oppression and even heavier taxation.

Key administrative posts were given to non-Jews or Hellenist Jews. He appointed as High Priest only those who would serve him faithfully, often from the Hellenist diaspora. The priests were subservient to the High Priest, so politics, and not religion, became the guiding light of many of them, leading to the corruption to which both Jesus and Josephus Flavius refer.

Herod built the port and city of Caesarea, through which silks and spices from the Far East were shipped to the Roman Empire. Control of this trade generated the revenue to finance the building of palaces and fortresses throughout the country, many of which have since been exposed by archaeological excavations.

The pride of Herod's accomplishments – the extension of, and the buildings on, the Temple Mount, including further enhancement of the Temple itself – were destroyed by the Romans in the year 70 CE, as was all that he built in Jerusalem. Only the western wall (the kotel) remains.

Herod married five times. Antipater, his son by his first wife, he executed shortly before he died. He also murdered his second wife, Miriamne, grand-daughter of Hyrcanus II, and their two sons Aristobolus IV and Alexander. His third wife was Miriamne, daughter of Simon the High Priest.

With Herod's death in 4 BCE his kingdom was divided between his sons. Archelaus inherited Judaea, Idumea and Samaria. His brother Herod Antipas inherited the Galilee and the Peraea (Jewish Transjordan) and their half-brother Philip inherited the Golan and the north-east part of the kingdom.

Avdat – a Nabatean caravan of camels
bringing silk and spices
across the desert.

Division of Herod's Kingdom 4 BCE

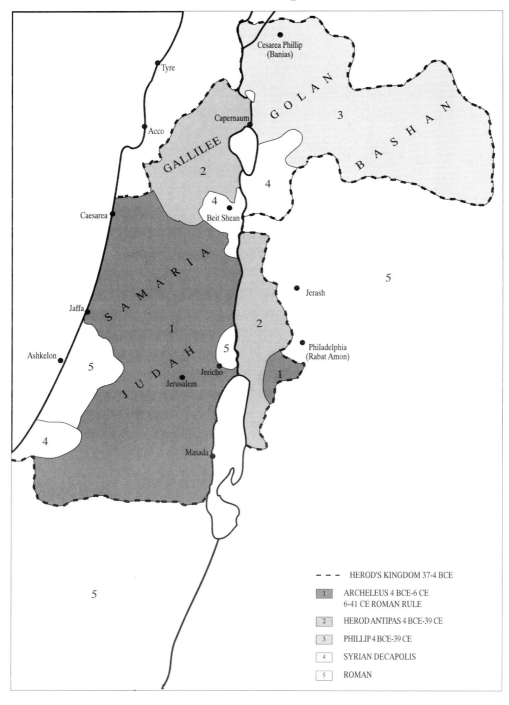

Cesarea Phillip
(Banias)

Tyre

G O L A N

Acco

Capernaum

B A S H A N

GALLILEE
2

3

4

Caesarea

4
Beit Shean

Jerash

S A M A R I A

5

Jaffa

1

2

Ashkelon

5

Philadelphia
(Rabat Amon)

J U D A H

5

1

Jericho
Jerusalem

4

Masada

5

- - - HEROD'S KINGDOM 37-4 BCE

[1] ARCHELEUS 4 BCE-6 CE
6-41 CE ROMAN RULE

[2] HEROD ANTIPAS 4 BCE-39 CE

[3] PHILLIP 4 BCE-39 CE

[4] SYRIAN DECAPOLIS

[5] ROMAN

About this time Joseph and Mary left Nazareth where they lived, to go to Bethlehem because of a census which the Romans had ordered. Here Jesus was born.

Archelaus was deposed by Rome in 6 CE and his domain became a Roman province known as Judaea. The capital was moved from Jerusalem to Caesarea where the prefect and later procurator resided. Judaea was no more than a satellite of the province of Syria where the bulk of the Roman army was stationed.

The Sanhedria in Jerusalem continued to serve as the highest authority in matters of religion but no longer had the right to try capital cases, as is borne out by John (18:31).

Dissatisfaction with Roman rule increased during the procuratorship of Pontius Pilate (26-36 CE), who deliberately refused to show tolerance for the Jewish religious susceptibilities. He minted coins with pagan cultic symbols and plundered the Temple treasury. There were numerous clashes between the Jewish population and the Roman legionnaires including one such clash mentioned by Luke (13:1).

Herod's family tomb – note the rolling stone door.

Herod Antipas ruled Galilee and Peraea. In Galilee he founded the city of Tiberias, which he named in honour of his patron Tiberius. Generally he was sensitive to the requirements of his Jewish population. However, it was he who, at the request of his step-daughter Salome, executed John the Baptist who preached against his marriage to Herodias, the ex-wife of his half-brother Philip.

All that we know of Jesus and his ministry comes to us from the New Testament which was canonised in the second half of the fourth century. Made up of twenty seven books, these do not appear in the order in which they were written.

Of the three Synoptic Gospels (gospel = evangelium = good news), it was thought that Mark was the earliest, in the third quarter of the first century, and that Matthew and Luke appeared to have used Mark as a source. However, there is a new school of thought which holds that perhaps Luke is the earlier source. John was written in the last decade of the first century and may have used Mark and Luke but is more theological than the Synoptic Gospels.

Luke is presumed to have also written the Book of Acts, which deals mainly with the lives of Peter and Paul. John is presumed to have also written the Book of Revelation, which is an eschatological prophesy. The remaining twenty one books are letters, about half of them written by Paul, describing the early church and its developing theology.

In the wake of the discovery of the hull of a two thousand year old boat, modern replicas sail on the Kinneret, the sea of Galilee.

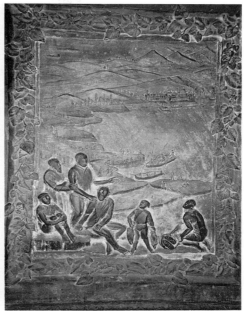

Above: Panels on the door of the Church of Tabgha, depicting scenes from the life of Jesus.

Right: The altar at the Mensa Christi Church.

Below:The altar in the Church of the Miracle of the Multiplication at Tabgha.

Until the end of the 19th century the King James Bible was the best known English translation. It was based on the Latin Vulgate and Greek manuscripts. With the discovery of even earlier manuscripts, new translations have corrected errors and modernised the language.

Although the gospels do not give dates for Jesus' ministry, it is usually placed between the years 28 and 30 CE. Most of the disciples of Jesus were fishermen in the Kinneret (the Sea of Galilee). He grew up, preached and performed most of His miracles in the Galilee where the sites were hallowed by His followers.

Judaea was governed by Pontius Pilate, so, when visiting Jerusalem, as a Galilean, Jesus was technically in a foreign country. At the time of Jesus' trial, Herod Antipas was visiting Jerusalem, which was not within his jurisdiction, even though Jesus was one of his subjects.

The authority of the High Priest and the Sanhedrin was limited to matters relating to religious laws. The authority of Pontius Pilate was paramount. Crucifixion was a punishment used frequently by the Romans.

Understanding the historical background of the period and visiting the places mentioned can give a new dimension and deeper understanding of the gospels.

The Crusader entrance to the Church of the Holy Sepulchre, also know as the Church of the Resurrection.

Philip died in 34 CE and the area he ruled was incorporated into the province of Syria. In 37 CE it was assigned by Caligula, the new emperor, to his friend Agrippa I, grandson of Herod and Mariamne, son of the murdered Aristobolus IV. Agrippa I was proclaimed king, and in 39 CE he received the domain of Herod Antipas, who was exiled to Gaul.

Agrippa was an able statesman and succeeded in dissuading Caligula from his plan to place a golden statue of himself in the Temple in Jerusalem. He was also instrumental in assuring the Senate's support for Claudius, who was proclaimed Emperor by the army after the assassination of Caligula.

As a token of gratitude Judaea and Samaria were added to his kingdom which now encompassed all the areas ruled by his grandfather, Herod. With his death in 44, his son Agrippa II continued as king but Judaea reverted to Roman rule under a procurator. Throughout the rule of Nero (54-68), Rome was in turmoil and each procurator was worse than his predecessor. The people were oppressed and overtaxed.

Josephus Flavius described the division in the Jewish population. There were the followers of the aristocratic Sadducees, the priestly cast, who were dependant on the Romans for their positions. The Pharisees and their followers were interested in safeguarding Jewish religious belief and practice and their attitude to Rome was moderate.

Virulently anti-Roman were the various zealot groups, whose aim was to expel the Romans and gain complete independence. They were able to gain support by promising the masses social reforms.

Last, but not least, there were the Essenes, about whom we learn from the Dead Sea Scrolls. They had separated themselves from both the Sadducees and the Pharisees, believing that Judaism and the Temple had become corrupt. "Sons of Light" is how they defined themselves. They used a different calendar and celebrated the festivals on a different date from the main body of Jews.

Unrest was widespread and a general revolt was a matter of time. The immediate cause was a series of events which began when Jews and pagans clashed in Caesarea. Rioting spread to Jerusalem. Agrippa II tried to restore order but the riots spread throughout the province.

Excavation at Qumran.

The Romans assembled a large force and marched against Jerusalem but were repulsed by the fury of the crowds. This limited victory encouraged more people to follow the banner of the revolt.

Nero sent Vespasian with an army of 60,000 to quell the revolt. Galilee was subdued, including the fortress at Jotpata. The commander of Jotpata, Joseph ben Mattathias, surrendered to Vespasian and eventually became a Roman citizen and court historian, known to us as Josephus Flavius.

Much of what we know about the great revolt, as well as about the history of the Jewish people from the Hasmonean revolt up to his times, is preserved in the books he wrote.

In a short time the Romans completed the conquest of Judaea but the upheaval in Rome, due to Nero's death in 68 CE, delayed the final blow to Jerusalem.

Vespasian was recalled to Rome and declared emperor. When he had restored law and order he sent his son Titus to complete the campaign against Jerusalem.

The various factions in Jerusalem had not utilized the interlude to formulate a joint defence plan. Titus attacked from the north, breached the third and then the second walls, besieged the Antonia fortress, razed it and, on the 9th day of the month of Av the Temple was taken and immediately destroyed. Within a short time the rest of the city fell. So thorough was the Roman destruction of Jerusalem that it burned for days – proof of which can today be seen in excavations.

The last places still holding out were Machaerus, on the eastern shore of the Dead Sea, and Masada, on the western side. According to Josephus, the people of Machaerus were tricked into surrendering.

The defenders of Masada, lead by Yair ben Eleazar, decided after three years siege, to "die unenslaved" by their enemies. When the Romans completed their final assault they were confronted with rows of dead bodies. They "did not exalt over them as enemies but admired the nobility of their resolve". (The Jewish War – Josephus Flavius).

These events bring to a close the second temple period and with it the end of Jewish autonomy. During the next two millenia Jews will mourn the destruction of the Temple and pray to be able to return to Jerusalem. Those who do, will pray at the Kotel, the western wall, also known as the Wailing Wall.

Robinson's Arch at the southern end of the western supporting wall
of the Herodian Temple Mount enclosure.

Chapter 6

Mishnah and Talmud
70–633

*A*lthough historically we remain in the Roman-pagan period, we are using a new chapter heading, for this is the period in which the Oral Law, companion to the biblical laws of the Torah, was codified.

As thorough as the Roman destruction was, by the beginning of the second century there appears to have been a substantial recovery. Towns and villages were rebuilt and agriculture revived. The only thing never to grow again in the land of Israel were the persimmons of Ein Gedi, destroyed together with the secret of producing their famous balsam.

With the loss of the Temple there was a feeling of despair as to the future of Jewish traditional life which was so dependant on the Temple and its rituals. To Rabbi Jochanan Ben Zakkai goes the credit for reestablishing Jewish communal life.

Deputy head of the Sanhedrin, he had escaped from Jerusalem in 70 CE. He was detained by the Romans at Yavneh (one of the places to which those who had surrendered to the Romans were taken) and there he revived the Sanhedrin and opened an academy. From there he proclaimed the sighting of the new moon, an important element in setting the dates of festivals, as the Jewish calendar is lunar.

Following in his wake, eminent sages and rabbis set up their houses of study throughout the country. It was in the Beit Midrash (academy) of Rabbi Akiva in Bnei Brak that the Passover Haggadah was finalized. In a sense this replaced the sacrificial and pilgrimage rituals of Pesach celebration in the time of the Temple.

During the rule of Trajan there was a Jewish revolt in Mesopotamia, 115-117 CE, ruthlessly suppressed by Lucius Quietus. This was a foreshadow of events to come. A decade later, during a visit to the east, Hadrian decided to make Jerusalem a pagan city and among other restrictions forbade circumcision.

A revolt led by Bar Kochba, with the support of Rabbi Akiva, broke out. The little we know of this revolt comes mainly from the Roman historian Dio Cassius and from archaeological excavations. Galilee was subdued earlier on, but in Judaea, coins minted in "year four of the redemption of Israel" were found.

The last fortress to fall, in 135 CE, was Betar. The revolt, coming a mere 62 years after the great revolt, was so intense that the Romans had to send

reinforcements from all over the empire. Their losses were so great that Dio Cassius wrote that Hadrian, in his dispatch to the Senate, refrained from using the customary introduction "... I and my troops are well".

Judaea lay in waste, its population sold into slavery. The Romans built a new city on the ruins of Jerusalem, naming it Aelia Capitolina, after the emperor Aelius Adrianus, but this new name did not stick. The name of the province was also changed, from Judaea to Syria-Palestina, an appellation in use, in one form or another, until the establishment of the State of Israel in 1948.

Ecce Homo arch, originally built by Hadrian.

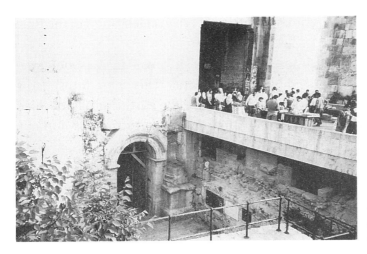

Remains of the Roman gate under the present Damascus gate.

An entire generation of sages perished in the Roman persecutions that followed, including Rabbi Shimon Bar Yochai, in whose memory the festival of Lag B'Omer is celebrated.

The Sanhedrin moved to Galilee, first to Usha then to Beit Shearim (c170), to Sepphoris (c200) and finally to Tiberias (c235). With the rise to power of the Severan dynasty in Rome, the persecution of Jews diminished.

Beit Shearim Catacomb. Inscriptions on sarcophagi indicate that people from as far away as the Greek islands chose to be buried here, the last resting place of Judah haNasi, redactor of the Mishnah.

Synagogue at Katzerin.

Rabbi Judah ha'Nasi (the Prince) who lead the Sanhedrin, was instrumental in the redaction of the Mishnah (c200).

The Mishnah is divided into six orders which are in turn divided into tractates. The Oral laws (halachah) which are derived from the biblical commandments, evolved over the centuries and the Mishnah preserves the discussions and controversies of its formative period.

Halachot not included in the Mishnah are known as the Tosefta and still later discussions are the Gemara. The Mishna, Tosefta and Gemara together form the basis for the Talmud.

The Jerusalem Talmud was finally redacted c 350 and is a commentary on, and an elaboration, clarification and updating of, the Mishnah. It concentrates on those halachot (laws) relevant to life in the Holy Land.

A page of the Talmud. The first two and a half lines of the central panel are the Mishnah. The continuation is the Gemara. The framing columns are later commentaries.

The Babylonian Talmud, a parallel development in the diaspora, emphasizes those halachot relevant to life in exile from the Holy Land. It was redacted about a century later.

Despite attempts to prevent Jews from referring to the Talmud and even public burnings of the Talmud, it will continue to serve as a guide to Jews all over the world in their day-to-day lives. It records the sayings and rulings of the Sages but is at the same time one of the most comprehensive legal codices in the world, and is studied not only by orthodox Jews.

A revised Hebrew addition updates the Talmud with the addition of commmentaries and footnotes which explain the Aramaic and sometimes archaic Hebrew. An English translation makes the Talmud available even to those who know no Hebrew. However, as with the Hebrew Scriptures, much is lost in the translation from Hebrew.

The English translation relates only to the first five lines of the previous photograph.

עו ע"א   CHAPTER SIX   76A

TRANSLATION AND COMMENTARY

[76A] ¹On the other hand, **if the employer retracts and dismisses the workers after they have begun the work for which they have been hired, he is at a disadvantage.** Accordingly, if wages have risen since the workers were first hired, the employer must pay them as agreed for the part of the work they have done. If, however, wages have fallen, he must pay the workers the full amount he originally promised them, less whatever he will now have to pay new workers to complete the task. ²The Mishnah concludes with two general rules: **Whoever deviates** from the terms of an agreement between an employer and a worker **is at a disadvantage.** For example, if someone brings wool to a dyer to be dyed red and he dyes it black, the dyer is not entitled to his full wages because he deviated from the agreement between the two parties. In such a case, the dyer is entitled either to the expenses he incurred in dyeing the wool black or to the value he added to the wool, whichever is less. ³Likewise, **whoever retracts** — this expression is explained by the Gemara below, 77b — **is at a disadvantage.**

GEMARA חָזְרוּ זֶה בָּזֶה לֹא קָתָנֵי ⁴The Gemara begins its discussion with an analysis of the first clause of the Mishnah, which stated that if workers are hired and one party misleads the other, the misled party has grounds for resentment against the other party but cannot press a monetary claim against him. The Gemara first wishes to determine the nature of the deception referred to in the Mishnah. It notes that **the Mishnah does not state** that "**one or the other retracted,**" which we would have understood as referring to a situation where the employer dismissed the workers or the workers refused to work, ⁵but rather the Mishnah states that **they misled each other.** Since the Mishnah does not speak of the parties *retracting,* but of *misleading* each other, it must be referring to a case where one party misled the other about the terms of employment. Now, assuming that the Mishnah is dealing with deception rather than retraction, the case is not one where the employer misled the workers or vice versa, but rather where **the workers** themselves **misled each other,** presumably by misrepresenting among themselves the terms of employment offered by the employer.

LITERAL TRANSLATION

[76A] ¹If the employer (lit., "the householder") retracts, he is at a disadvantage. ²Whoever deviates is at a disadvantage, ³and whoever retracts is at a disadvantage.

GEMARA ⁴[The Mishnah] does not state: "And one or the other retracted," ⁵but: "And they misled each other," [implying] that the *workers* misled each other.

[76A] ¹ אִם בַּעַל הַבַּיִת חוֹזֵר בּוֹ, יָדוֹ עַל הַתַּחְתּוֹנָה. ² כָּל הַמְשַׁנֶּה יָדוֹ עַל הַתַּחְתּוֹנָה, ³ וְכָל הַחוֹזֵר בּוֹ יָדוֹ עַל הַתַּחְתּוֹנָה.

גמרא ⁴ "חָזְרוּ זֶה בָּזֶה" לֹא קָתָנֵי, ⁵ אֶלָּא: "הִטְעוּ זֶה אֶת זֶה", דְּאַטְעוּ פּוֹעֲלִים אַהֲדָדֵי.

RASHI

אם בעל הבית חוזר בו ידו על התחתונה — מפרש לקמן מה טעם. וסד כל המשנה ידו על התחתונה — כגון נתן צמר לצבע לצבעו אדום וצבעו שחור, אם השבח יתר על היציאה — נותן לו סכר כפחותם, מוך ממה שהוציא להוציאה כסלאחת — נותן לו השבח. גמרא חזרו בהן בו קתני — נעושה הלי "הטעו" סם את בעל הבית או בעל הבית אותם, דאם כן היכי קמני "למיחני" במאי מורי. דאטעו פועלים אהדדי — אחד מן הפועלים הטעה את חבירו.

NOTES

אם בעל הבית חוזר בו **If the employer retracts.** Our commentary follows *Rashi,* who explains that the employer is always at a disadvantage, regardless of whether labor costs increase or decrease. Specifically, if wages rise, the employer must pay the workers for the work they have done according to the rate that was originally promised them, even though it will now cost him more to finish the work. And if wages fall, the employer must pay the workers what he originally stipulated, minus whatever is necessary to complete the work.
Other commentators, however, maintain that the employer is only "at a disadvantage" if wages rise (as explained above); but if wages fall, he need pay them only for the work they have done at the rate promised — for if he were required to pay the workers their full salary minus the cost of completing the work, he would then end up paying them more than the actual value of their work (*Talmud Rabbenu Peretz* in the name of *Ri*).

חָזְרוּ זֶה בָּזֶה לֹא קָתָנֵי, אֶלָּא הִטְעוּ זֶה אֶת זֶה **The Mishnah does not state: "And one or the other retracted," but: "And they misled each other."** The Gemara assumes that the Mishnah is referring to a case where one of the workers misled the others, because it seems to have had difficulty in constructing a case where the workers or the employer misled each other. The Jerusalem Talmud, however, interprets the Mishnah as referring to a case where the workers misled the employer or vice versa when negotiating the terms of employment. The workers told the employer that most other workers earn ten zuz a day when in fact they are paid only five zuz, or the employer told the the workers that the standard pay is five zuz a day when in fact workers earn ten. According to the Jerusalem Talmud, the Mishnah rules that in either case the agreement is binding and the party misled has grounds for resentment only. Indeed, *Ra'avad* asks why our Gemara did not explain the Mishnah the same way as did the Jerusalem Talmud, since

Byzantine Period   333–633

In 313 CE Constantine recognized the Christian religion and at the end of his reign declared it to be one of the official religions of the Roman Empire. Monotheism slowly replaced paganism in the western world.

Queen Helena, mother of Constantine visited the Holy Land and ordered the building of churches on the sites of events recorded by the gospels. The first were in Bethlehem, birthplace of Jesus, and in Jerusalem, site of His crucifixion, burial and ascension.

Churches were also built in Galilee and Judaea to commemorate the miracles performed there. In Jerusalem the churches follow Jesus' footsteps during his last days and hours. The forty pentecostal days too, are recalled.

Pater Noster in Hebrew and English.

Almost all of these churches will be destroyed by the Persian and Moslem conquerors. Some will be rebuilt by the Crusaders and again destroyed by the Moslem conquerors. Many will become the venue of pilgrims in the 19th and 20th centuries, when modern churches are built.

Upheavals in the Roman Empire resulted in a split between the western and eastern parts. Throughout the eastern Byzantine Empire the position of the Jews deteriorated due to discriminatory laws. In Palestine they lost autonomous control of their religious affairs and were forbidden to proclaim the advent of the new moon.

Based on astronomical research and records the calendar was fixed in 358 CE and was dispatched to all diaspora communities. It is still in use today.

Among those who visit the Holy Land, and leave us with tantalizing descriptions, are the anonymous pilgrim from Bordeaux in 333 CE and the nun Egeria in 381-4 CE. Eusebius wrote the Onamasticion, an invaluable list of towns and place names. St. Jerome, who lived in Bethlehem at the end of 4th century, translated the scriptures into Latin. Known as the Vulgate, this became the basis for the early translations into English.

Palestina thrived. From archaeological excavations we know that there was a large Jewish population living side by side with Christians – as seen by synagogues and churches. Agriculture flourished. Its by-products, such as oil, wine, linen, etc, were highly thought of in western markets.

In the 6th century, when the Roman Empire was invaded by the Visigoths, Huns and Vandals, Christian ascetics made their way to the Holy Land. Some lived in isolation in caves, others lived in small groups and yet others in monasteries. Most were in the Judaean Desert. The oldest intact monastery is St. Catherine's in Sinai which has an unexplored library of centuries-old unique manuscripts.

In 614 CE the Persians set out to conquer the disintegrating Byzantine Empire and the Jews joined them, hoping to throw off Christian oppression. The Persians captured Jerusalem and destroyed many churches through the land. In 629 CE the tables were turned and Heraclius restored the relics of the true cross to its rightful place in the Church of the Holy Sepulchre, but not for long.

Events in the Arabian Desert are going to bring changes to the Christian world, which at this point in history stretched from the Fertile Crescent through Asia Minor and Egypt to Europe.

Jerusalem as depicted on the floor of the Byzantine monastery at Medba in Jordan.

| Chapter 7 | # Early Arab
633–1099 |

W̶ritten sources relating to the Holy Land in this period are scant and we have to rely on historical events taking place elsewhere.

After the Persian conquest in 614 CE, Emperor Heraclius restored the Christian holy sites to Christian rule for a very short period. However the threat was no longer Persia. A new monotheistic religion had begun in the Arabian peninsula, birthplace of Mohammed, and by 634 CE Islam had swept through a large part of the Christian Byzantine world – the Fertile Crescent (Syria, Babylon), the Holy Land, Asia Minor (Turkey), Egypt and on to North Africa and even Spain.

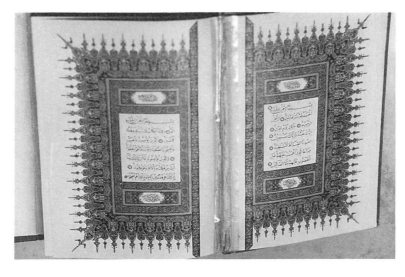

Illuminated opening pages of the Koran.

Spread of Islam

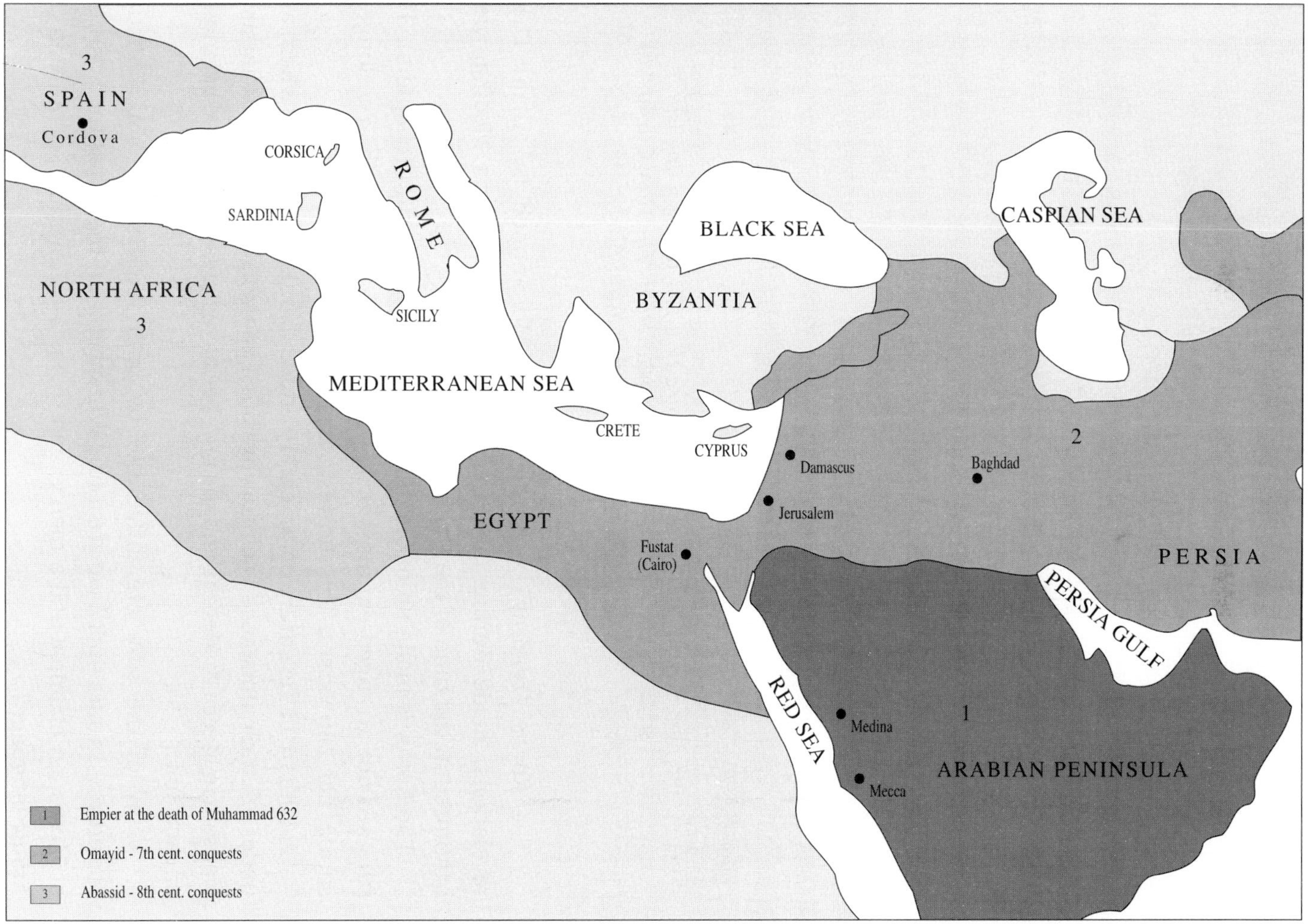

CASPIAN SEA

PERSIA

PERSIA GULF

ARABIAN PENINSULA

2

Baghdad

1

BLACK SEA

BYZANTIA

Damascus

Jerusalem

Medina

Mecca

RED SEA

CYPRUS

Fustat
(Cairo)

CRETE

EGYPT

MEDITERRANEAN SEA

ROME

SICILY

CORSICA

SARDINIA

NORTH AFRICA

3

SPAIN

Cordova

3

1	Empier at the death of Muhammad 632
2	Omayid - 7th cent. conquests
3	Abassid - 8th cent. conquests

S. IV. 171-173.]

Christ Jesus the son of Mary
Was (no more than)
An apostle of God,
And His Word,
Which He bestowed on Mary,
And a Spirit proceeding
From Him : so believe
In God and His apostles.
Say not " Trinity " : desist : [676]
It will be better for you :
For God is One God :
Glory be to Him :
(Far Exalted is He) above
Having a son. To Him
Belong all things in the heavens
And on earth. And enough
Is God as a Disposer of affairs.

SECTION 24.

172. Christ disdaineth not
To serve and worship God,[677]
Nor do the angels, those
Nearest (to God) :
Those who disdain
His worship and are arrogant,—
He will gather them all
Together unto Himself [678]
To (answer).

173. But to those who believe
And do deeds of righteousness,
He will give their (due)
Rewards,—and more,
Out of His bounty :
But those who are
Disdainful and arrogant,
He will punish

676. Christ's attributes are mentioned : (1) that he was the son of a woman, Mary, and therefore a man ; (2) but an apostle, a man with a mission from God, and therefore entitled to honour ; (3) a Word bestowed on Mary, for he was created by God's word "Be" (*kun*), and he was ; iii. 59 ; (4) a spirit proceeding from God, but not God : his life and his mission were more limited than in the case of some other apostles, though we must pay equal honour to him as a man of God. The doctrines of Trinity, equality with God, and sonship, are repudiated as blasphemies. God is independent of all needs and has no need of a son to manage His affairs. The Gospel of John (whoever wrote it) has put in a great deal of Alexandrian and Gnostic mysticism round the doctrine of the Word (Greek, Logos), but it is simply explained here, and our §§fis work on this explanation.

677. Christ often watched and prayed, as a humble worshipper of God ; and his agony in the Garden of Gethsemane was full of human dignity, suffering, and self-humiliation (see Matt. xxvi. 36-45).

678. The disdainful and the arrogant are the crew of Satan, who will be gathered together before the Supreme Throne for punishment.

Sura IV v 171 from an English translation of "The Holy Qur-an" by Abdullah Yusuf Ali.

The Koran (reading) was revealed to Mohammed by Allah. These revelations, made during the Prophet's life in Mecca and Medina, were canonised in the time of the Caliph Othman, c 651.

The Koran is made up of one hundred and fourteen sura (chapters). The sura are not arranged chronologically but according to length. The longest, sura 2, has 286 verses. The shortest, sura 114, has 4 verses.

A 10th or 11th century commentary added details as to where, when, and under what circumstance each sura was first spoken. The subject, whether it was said in Mecca or Medina and the number of verses, appear at the beginning of each sura.

Many of the sura are influenced by both the Hebrew and Christian Scriptures. In sura 46:12 we are told: "When before it there was the Scripture of Moses, an example and a mercy; and this is a confirming Scripture in the Arabic language".

The Koran has not been as widely translated as the Bible because of the belief that the contents cannot be accurately expressed in any language other than Arabic.

Sura 1 is the prayer which devout Moslems say five times a day, usually repeated between five and seven times, accompanied by kneeling and prostrating (rak'a). This is always said in Arabic.

Only on Friday, at the second prayer of the day, are Moslems obliged to go to a mosque. The prayer (rak'a) is repeated twelve times and a sermon (hutba) is given on religious or topical subjects.

With the sudden death of Mohammed in 632 CE, two groups contest for the leadership, which includes secular matters such as control of the army and empire, as well as religious matters. One group, led by Abu Bakr, followed the way (sunna) of Mohammed. The other, led by Mohammed's nephew and son-in-law, Ali, believed that the leadership should come from the "tent of the prophet", his direct descendants.

Both Ali, and his son, Mohammed's grandson, Hussein were murdered. Their followers decide to become a separate group (shi'a) whose spiritual leader, Imam, will always be a descendant of Mohammed.

About 90% of the world's Moslems are Sunni including those in the Holy Land. The Druze, Alawi and Bahai are all offshoots of the Shiites.

Under the first Caliphs the seat of power was Mecca, but then it moved to Damascus under the Omayyid dynasty (638-750 CE). During this period the Holy Land thrived as can be seen from the archaeological remains of palaces in Jerusalem and Jericho. In 750 CE the (Sunni) Omayyids were overthrown by the (Shiite) Abassids and the centre of power shifted to Baghdad.

One of the notable Abassid Caliphs, Haroun al Rashid (783-809 CE), made an alliance with Charlemagne of France (later to become Holy Roman Emperor) and presented him with the keys to the Church of the Resurrection which was under Moslem control.

The Abassid hegemony was disrupted in the 10th century with the creation of the (Shiite) Fatimid Caliphate in Egypt which extended its rule to include the Holy Land and destroyed many churches. During the rule of Al Hakim (996-1021 CE) a group broke away from the Ismailia Shiites.

Persecuted in Egypt in the 18th century, they eventually settled in the remote hills of Galilee, Golan Heights and Syria. Known as Druze, they practised a secret religion, which has no similarity to Islam, and venerated their prophet at the tomb of Nebi Shueb.

The population of the Holy Land continued to decrease, agriculture diminishing, vineyards destroyed. Absentee land-owners taxed the peasants who barely eked out a living. Desolation and lawlessness prevailed, travel was dangerous, pilgrims were attacked. The rivalry between the Caliphates made the Holy Land ripe for Crusader conquest.

The Dome of the Rock, built on the Temple Mount in Jerusalem, is the best known site of the Early Arab period. Built in 691 CE by Omayyid Caliph Aba al Malik, it was a memorial honouring the rock on which it was built, the rock from which Mohammed ascended to heaven. According to the legend, the Rock tried to ascend with him only to be pushed back by the angel Gabriel and visitors are shown Mohammed's foot print and the imprint of Gabriel's hand.

The inspiration for the design of the Dome of the Rock was the rotunda of the nearby Byzantine Church of the Resurrection. The dome, which collapsed in 1016, has been repaired many times, gold leafed in 1962 and again in 1994. The facade tiles have been replaced, but the original structure is unchanged.

Dome of the Rock.

The interior is decorated with geometric and floral patterns and inscriptions in stylised Arabic, mainly from the Koran. Abassid Caliph al Mamun erased the name of al Malik, the builder, and replaced it with his own. Because he omitted to change the date, his forgery was exposed.

There is no mention of Jerusalem in the Koran. In the verses referring to Mohammed's night flight on his horse, el Burak, the destination is given as El Aksa (the furthest) Mosque, originally thought to have been heaven.

The Omayyids, who moved the centre of Islamic rule to Damascus, needed a Moslem pilgrimage site to compete with Mecca and Medina. At this point the "Furthest Mosque" was redefined as Jerusalem, already holy to Jews and Christians.

Caliph al Walid 709-715 CE built the El Aksa Mosque at the southern end of the Temple Mount on the site of the Byzantine Church of St. Mary. This mosque underwent many changes and even served as a church in the Crusader period.

Mosque at Ramla.

Hisham's palace in Jericho.

In Philip Hittis's book "Great Arab Cities" these two sites, the Dome of the Rock and the El Aksa Mosque, are the only ones mentioned in the entire Holy Land area. Jerusalem, however, did not gain religious importance in Islamic tradition and did not become a major pilgrimage site.

Although there is no record of the Omayyid palace outside the southern wall of the Temple Mount, archaeological excavations have uncovered this previously unknown luxurious complex.

A short distance from Jericho another Omayyid palace, Khirbet Mafjer, has been excavated. Built by the Caliph Hisham ibn Abed el Malikh (724-743 CE) and razed by an earthquake, probably before it was much used, the beautiful mosaics and many statues of human and animal figures, indicate a pre-iconoclastic (destruction of images) period in Moslem art.

The masons' symbols on the stones are in Hebrew, indicating Jewish builders. The remains of the "Shalom al Israel" synagogue close by confirm that there was a large Jewish population in the vicinity.

At this time Arabic was introduced as an official language, alongside Greek which, in a short time, was no longer used.

The importance of Jerusalem declined – in fact only two Abassid Caliphs visited Jerusalem. The area west of the Jordan river was now known as Jund Falastin (a corruption of the Byzantine Palestina) and its administrative capital was the new town of Ramla, built in 718 CE on the main trade route between Egypt and Damascus.

Mukadasi described the minaret built by Hisham and defined the mihrab as the most beautiful in all Islam. Sections of the intricate water system have been excavated.

From documents found in the Genizah in Cairo we know that there was a flourishing Karaite community and at least two synagogues in Ramla.

Ezrah Synagogue in Cairo.

Chapter 8

Crusader Period
1099–1287

The rivalry between Fatamid Egypt and the Seljuk Turks for the control of the Holy Land resulted in a power vacuum. Together with obstacles placed in the way of Christian pilgrims, the stage was set for the Crusader conquest.

In Europe too there was upheaval. Independent kings and princes were constantly at war with one another. In an attempt to unify Europe (which, together with England, was Catholic) the Pope called for a combined crusade to free the Christian holy places from the infidel. Pope Urban II had another motive – to force the Byzantine Empire (which was Orthodox) to recognise Rome as the leader of the Christian world.

Who were the crusaders who answered this call? On one hand feudal knights, usually the third son, who could not inherit family property in Europe and England, with nothing to lose and perhaps honour to gain. On the other hand, the peasants and rabble, unemployed and starving in many cases. They had everything to gain including a church pardon for all sins, past, present and future.

It is doubtful if the Crusaders ever comprised more than 25% of the population in the areas they conquered in the Holy Land.

The local population consisted mainly of:

1. Arab peasants who leased the land from absentee landlords and, after paying taxes, barely eked out a living (Arabs in the cities were slaughtered by the conquering crusaders)

2. Jews in towns and villages throughout the land

Crusader Kingdoms

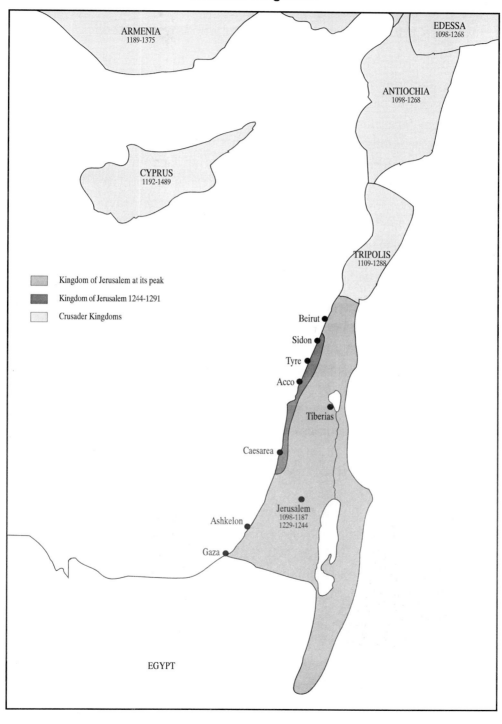

ARMENIA
1189-1375

EDESSA
1098-1268

ANTIOCHIA
1098-1268

CYPRUS
1192-1489

TRIPOLIS
1109-1288

Kingdom of Jerusalem at its peak

Kingdom of Jerusalem 1244-1291

Crusader Kingdoms

Beirut

Sidon

Tyre

Acco

Tiberias

Caesarea

Jerusalem
1098-1187
1229-1244

Ashkelon

Gaza

EGYPT

3.   Various Christian communities, none of whom were Catholic.

During their rule, the Crusaders stepped into the place of the absentee landlords and imposed European feudal law which probably improved the conditions of the peasants. The Jewish population was persecuted and even banned from Jerusalem.

No close relations were formed with the local Christian population. Often the Crusaders replaced the Greek Orthodox, Syrian Jacobite, Armenian, Coptic and Ethiopian Bishops and clergy with Latin (Catholic) prelates. Instead of a Christian alliance, these groups even saw Saladin as their saviour.

The demise of Crusader rule was partly due to the lack of unity among the crusaders themselves. But their final expulsion was due to the changes in the area.

Between 1095 and 1297 there were a number of Crusades to the Holy Land. Not all of them reached its shores. The 1st Crusade (1095-99) established princedoms in Antiochia and Edessa and, under Tancred and Godfrey de Bouillon, the first king, finally conquered Jerusalem in 1099.

William of Tyre described the conquest of Jerusalem: "It was impossible to look on the vast numbers of slain without horror. Everywhere lay fragments of human bodies and the ground was covered with the blood of the slain. Not only the spectacle of headless bodies and mutilated limbs strewn in all directions roused horror in all who looked upon them. Still more dreadful it was to gaze upon the victors themselves, dripping with blood from head to foot".

After the conquest of Jerusalem, many of the Crusaders returned to Europe. Baldwin succeeded Godfrey as king. Over the next forty years the Crusader kingdom consolidated and reached a modus vivendi with the Moslems of Damascus, who prefered an alliance with the Crusaders rather than one with Zengi of Mosul. (The Iraqis taunt the Syrians about this right up to the present!).

The fleets of Genoa, Venice and Pisa were offered concessions – customs exemptions and commerical monopolies – for their assistance. All the coastal cities down to Ashkelon in the south came under Crusader control.

Assisted by the Crusaders, the Damascenes repulsed Zengi. As a reward, Banias was ceded by the Syrians to the Crusaders. But this alliance didn't last long. Damascus fell to Nuradin, Zengi's heir.

Saladin, a Kurd from Iraq, became ruler of Egypt. The Crusader kingdom was a buffer zone between the two rivals – Nuradin and Saladin. Saladin's attempt to attack the kingdom of Jerusalem resulted in his defeat at the hands of Amalric and realisation that he had to unite the Moslems from North Africa to Turkey, Egypt, Aleppo and Damascus.

During this period the Crusaders did not reorganise and Europe sent no reinforcements. The fateful battle of the Horns of Hittin in July 1187 was the beginning of the end for the Crusader kingdom.

The Crusaders were at Sephoris (Zippori) when they heard of the fall of Tiberias. Count Reymond, a Hospitaller knight whose ancestors arrived on the 1st Crusade, urged his colleagues not to be lured into a battle where the

Crusader remains at Caesarea.

crusader army would be short of water. Gerard of Ridfort, a Templar and relative newcomer, convinced the weak Guy de Lusignan to attack at once to regain Tiberias.

Because Moslem horsemen were lightly armed they had more maneuverability than the heavily armoured mounted knights. The Crusaders set out for Tiberias but by afternoon had only covered eighteen kilometres. They had suffered heavy losses and were without water. Raymond suggested that the Crusaders detour immediately to the springs of Hittin, five kilometres away, in order to obtain water and regroup. Guy decided to set up camp and rest till morning.

This gave the Moslems ample time to reorganise their troops and to bring water and supplies from the rear, harassing the Crusaders all the while. In the morning the Crusaders tried to get to the Hittin Springs but Saladin succeeded

Crusader remains at Belvoir.

in separating the mounted knights from their protective shield of foot soldiers and then set fire to the dry grass.

The Crusaders fought valiantly but to no avail. The true cross, brought from Jerusalem, was captured; the leaders were imprisoned and the kingdom was now defenceless. In October 1187 Jerusalem fell to Saladin. The Crusader kingdom shrank to a narrow strip along the coastal plain.

In Europe the Third Crusade was mobilised, led by Frederick I, Phillip II and Richard the Lionhearted. Cyprus was conquered. In the Holy Land, Richard defeated Saladin at Arsuf and reestablished the kingdom of Jerusalem, but only for ten years.

The Fourth Crusade got no further than Constantinople. The Fifth resulted in an agreement with the Egyptian sultan. Then, due to hostility between the rulers of Egypt and Damascus, the Sixth Crusade succeeded in regaining

Crusader remains at Acco.

almost all of the Holy Land. After a short interlude it shrank once again to a narrow coastal strip.

The Mamelukes, slaves brought to serve the Egyptian sultan, overthrew their masters and gained control of Egypt, to the west. The Mongols, led by Genghis Khan, captured Damascus, to the north-east, and in their advance to Egypt were stopped at Ein Jalud ('Harod springs) in 1260 by the Mamelukes.

The crusaders were caught in between. Finally, in 1291, the Crusader kingdom was completely destroyed by the Mamelukes.

The Seventh, and last, Crusade, the Children's Crusade, didn't even leave the shores of Europe. The children either died or were sold as slaves.

Most of the Crusader remains, such as Belvoir, Caesarea and Montfort, throughout the country date to the final swan song of the Crusade Kingdom. Their size and majesty belie the fact that the Crusaders were overcome by internal disputes and lacked unity or a forceful command.

Churches which the Crusaders had built on the ruins of Byzantine churches (destroyed during the early Moslem rule) were destroyed by the new Moslem conquerers. Some architects have tried to incorporate these ruins in modern churches. Some examples are: the Church of the Multiplication at Tabgha; Church of the Annunciation in Nazareth; the Church of the Transfiguration on Mt. Tabor.

Crusader seal depicting scenes of Jerusalem.

Chapter 9

Mameluke Period
1297–1517

*T*he Mameluke period overlaps the end of the Crusader period, with its ever-decreasing kingdom. The Mamelukes were not a people or a nation. They were the descendants of pagan slaves brought from Asia Minor by the Caliphs of Egypt, to serve in their personal armies. In time they usurped power and became the rulers of Egypt.

In 1260 the Mamelukes under Sultan al Malik Beybers stopped the advance of Mongol tribes, united under Genghis Khan, at the battle of Ein Jalud (Ein

Crusader and Mameluke soldiers in the courtyard of the Citadel Museum in Jerusalem.

Harod). Syria came under Mameluke control and the Crusader kingdom was caught in between, shrinking until it was merely the coastal strip and then, finally, vanquished.

To prevent the return of the Crusaders, harbours were filled with the rubble of the razed cities and citadels. Beybers is quoted as saying: "Your ships are your horses and our horses are our ships".

This destruction led to the abandonment of entire areas.

The Mameluke capital, Cairo, was not in the centre of the empire, so an elaborate early warning system was devised. A report from northern Syria could reach Cairo in sixty hours. The road system was improved, bridges were built and a chain of khans, at regular intervals, were provided with relief horses. At the entrance to Lod one such bridge is still in use, with the engraving of a lion amusing itself with a mouse – the symbol used by Beybers.

Khan at Acco.

To counter the dangers of a new crusade and to control Christian pilgrims, the Islamic aspects of the province were emphasised. In Ramleh, the Great Mosque, which had been converted to a church, was renovated. The Red Mosque was built in Safed and residents of Damascus were encouraged to emigrate to Safed by gifts of fertile lands in the surrounding valleys.

The Cave of the Machpela (the tomb of the patriarchs and the matriarchs) in Hebron was renovated and entry to non-Moslems was barred – a ban which continued until 1967.

In order to express loyalty to Moslem culture, the Mamelukes built extensively in Jerusalem. All the buildings were consecrated to the Moslem authorities. In this way they safeguarded the future of their sons who, by law, were not allowed to inherit their father's rank, possessions or position.

Legally, the sultan was permitted to confiscate the possessions of a Mameluke for the state treasury. However, as no sultan could confiscate holy endowments, by appointing their sons as trustees of property bequeathed to the Wakf (Moslem religious authorities), they were thereby guaranteed a regular income. Their striking white, pink and black stone buildings can still be seen in the old city of Jerusalem.

Although they built beautifully, they did not govern well. Most of the time the country was in chaos and Bedouin tribes marauded at will. Travel was dangerous. The custom of wealth and influence being monopolised by a handful of families gained ground.

Officials in Damascus and Cairo, doubtless on receipt of a generous tribute from these families, authorised the acquisition of large land holdings and their appointment to the most influential political and religious offices in the province.

The beginning of the demise of the Mameluke Empire began in 1453, when Muhamed II of the expanding Ottoman Empire seized Constantinople and gained control of most of what was once the Byzantine Empire. The Ottoman Turks proceeded to usurp the Caliphate from the Mamelukes and by 1516 the Holy Land was formally under Ottoman rule.

Chapter 10

Ottoman Period
1516–1917

*O*nce again we see how events in other parts of the world affect the Holy Land. The Mongols, the Seljuks and now the Ottoman Turks, who exploited the power vacuum in what remained of the Byzantine Empire, penetrated western Europe. Their rule extended almost as far as Vienna, included the Balkans, eastern Europe, the Black Sea, North Africa, Egypt and Asia as far as Persia. Even the Moslem holy cities of Mecca and Medina recognised Ottoman control.

Suleiman the Magnificent, builder of the present-day walls of the Old City of Jerusalem, offered asylum to Jews who had been expelled in 1492 from Spain. Many of them made their way to Safed in the Galilee, which became the centre of kabala studies. For a short while, Tiberias thrived under the influence of Donna Gracia and her nephew Don Joseph Nasi.

France, the protector of the Catholic churches and holy places in the Holy Land, was the first to penetrate the Ottoman Empire as it began to weaken. Then the Russians became the protectors of the Orthodox churches throughout the Ottoman Empire.

For a short period in the mid-18th century, Daher el Omar took control of the Galilee area and improved the condition of the local population by developing agriculture and even encouraging Jewish settlement. He was overthrown by Ahmed Pasha el Jazzar who, assisted by his private army of Albanian, Bosnian and Circassian mercenaries, governed from Acco.

Lion's Gate and wall of the Old City.

In 1798, Napoleon invaded Egypt, realising that it was the key to the east. Continuing up the Mediterranean coast, the French reached Jaffa, where they offered terms of surrender. These were either rejected, resulting in wholesale looting and massacre, or were accepted and then ignored by the French who, due to manpower shortage, could not afford to use their meagre troops for guards and so marched the captives straight into the sea.

The French were beset by plagues but continued their conquests through Samaria and Galilee, hoping to advance to Constantinople and thus into Europe from the east. Unbeknown to them, el Jezzar of Acco was assisted by Col. Phillippe, a Frenchman who had been at the military academy with Napoleon, but was now fighting with the English.

The siege and assault on Acco failed and with the English fleet in the Mediterranean the French had no option but to retreat the way they had come – to Egypt and then back to France.

A little known proclamation issued by Napoleon, addressed to "the rightful heirs of Palestine" called on the "Israelites, unique nation, whom, in thousands of years, lust of conquest were able to deprive of the ancestral lands only, but not of name and national existence" to "claim the restoration of your rights among the population of the universe".

In 1831, Mohammed Ali extended Egypt's borders to include Palestine. In 1841, an alliance of England, Prussia, Austria and Turkey returned Palestine to the Ottoman Empire, which henceforth would be known as the "sick man of Europe".

One of the pretexts for the Crimean War (1853-56) related to guardianship of the Christian holy places in Palestine. Turkey declared war on Russia, the protector of the Orthodox Church. France, protector of the Catholic Church, and England, joined Turkey. In return, the western powers were henceforth going to be awarded "capitulations" in Palestine, which was slowly awakening from a six hundred year long deep sleep.

Most of the land throughout the Ottoman Empire belonged to the Sultan (Porte) who often put it at the disposal of an influential class of absentee landlords. In some areas pasturing and wood gathering was permitted to all, but this resulted in the deterioration of the quality of the soil. By and large the local Moslem population were peasants living in abject poverty and paying exhorbitant taxes to absentee landlords.

Jews lived mainly in Jerusalem, Hebron, Tiberias and Safed – known as the four holy cities – as well as in Jaffa, the only port of entry to Palestine. For many, their existence depended on donations from abroad, such as the support of Moses Montefiore (later Sir Moses), who built the first residential neighbourhood outside the walls of Jerusalem.

In 1864, in Springfield Massachusetts, a group of Christians led by George Jones Adams, decided to establish a colony in Palestine, there to await the second advent of the Messiah. One hundred and fifty three followers arrived in 1866 and the prefabricated houses they brought with them can still be seen in Jaffa, where they settled.

Unfortunately they were left destitute by their leader and Mark Twain, on a cruise in the Mediterranean, collected money from his companions to repatriate those who so desired. Only twenty-nine remained, and one of them would drive the first carriage on the first paved road.

Mark Twain described the land as "a desolate country whose soil is rich enough but is given over wholly to weeds … a silent mournful expanse … a desolation is here that not even imagination can grace with the pomp of life

American colony house in Jaffa.

and action ... even the olive and the cactus, those fast friends of a worthless soil have almost deserted the country" (The Innocents Abroad 1867).

At about the same time, another Christian group was organised in Germany for the same religious reason. Known as the Templars, they established a number of colonies, introduced modern agricultural equipment, constructed the first roads and signed a contract with Thomas Cook, thereby establishing the first travel agency in Palestine.

In 1868, the Bahu-Allah founder of the Bahai faith was exiled to Acco, where he is buried. The Bab, herald of the faith, was re-interned in Haifa. These shrines are regarded as Holy Places and are visited by Bahai pilgrims from all over the world.

The opening of the Suez Canal in 1869 put Palestine firmly on the tourist map thanks to the many VIP's who attended the opening ceremony and then continued to the Holy Land. The Ottoman Empire was obliged to invest first in the road from Jaffa to Jerusalem and then a road from the coast to Nazareth.

The very first wave of Jewish immigration is one which is generally forgotten – Jews from Yemen who made their way by foot, nourished by religious fervour.

After them came the East European Jews of the First Aliya (immigration). Members of different organisations encouraged the return of the Jewish people to the land where they had originated. Many were religious families.

Under the leadership of Theodore Herzl, representatives of these groups met at the first Zionist Congress in 1898 in Basel. There, Herzl prophesied that the Jews would have their own state within fifty years. "If you will it, it is no legend".

Money collected throughout the Jewish world helped to finance the purchase of land for the many settlements as well as for schools and even the beginnings of a bank. The farming colonies established then are towns of modern Israel – Rishon leZion, Petach Tikva, Rosh Pina, Zichron Ya'acov, to name but a few.

The land offered for sale was in uncultivated areas, mainly the valleys which more often than not were malaria-infested swamps. H.B. Tristram did not find " a sign of habitation in the valleys, even where the valley is wide and

While Jewish, Christian, Moslem, Druze and Bahai sites are familiar to many visitors, few know the Achmedian mosque in Haifa. Achmedians are Moslems who do not believe in religious war (Jihad).

suitable for cultivation ... a monotony of stagnation, devoid of life and movement." (The Land of Israel: A Journal of Travels in Palestine).

In many instances, it was the generosity of Baron Edmond Rothschild which helped the pioneers survive such hardships as shortage of water and illness. He was successful in reintroducing the wine industry to the Holy Land. The mulberry trees in Rosh Pina were to serve as a base for the silk farms, but this plan did not succeed.

In 1892, the first railway line was completed. Instead of it taking a full day to reach Jerusalem from Jaffa, it now took only a few hours. (It still takes a few hours to get to Jerusalem by train, following the same winding, scenic route. Even the Jerusalem railway station is unchanged!).

Turkey was interested in completing the Hejaz line to connect Turkey with the Moslem sites at Mecca and Medina. The various branch lines connecting Haifa, Tiberias, Beit Shean, Afula and on to Be'er Sheva' were important for the development of the country.

1904 saw the beginning of a new wave of immigration, the Second Aliya. This consisted mainly of young people, shocked by the Kishinev pogroms and disillusioned by the first Russian Revolution, but fired with the idea of socialism.

These were the pioneers who would establish the kibbutz and moshav movements and introduce a form of settlement based on a communal life style and mutual responsibility. Right up until today, people all over the world volunteer to work on a kibbutz in order to experience this unique way of life.

Wall of Old City. In the upper-right Church of the Dormition on Mount Zion.

Ein Gedi waterfall

The Dead Sea, 400 metres below sea level, 35% salt. In the distance, the mountains of Moab.

Massada looking east towards the Dead Sea.   The remains of the Roman ramp in the foreground.

Megiddo. Part of the water system originally built by the Canaanites and enlarged during the Israelite period.

Banias, also known as Caesarea Phillipi. Statues of pagan gods, including Pan, were displayed in the niches.

Tel Dan. A unique sun-baked mud brick Bronze Age gateway.

Dan river, one of the tributaries of the Jordan river.

Aerial view of the Old City of Jerusalem looking north. In the centre, the Temple Mount enclosure, site of the First and Second Temples. In foreground, the southern excavations, outside the Old City wall.

Zippori-Sephoris.
Part of the elaborate water
system of aquaducts and
underground reservoirs.

Sabra, the fruit of the cactus, is the name given to those born in Israel. The reason? Both are prickly on the outside but sweet inside.

The economic development in an island of stagnation caused Arabs from the neighbouring provinces of the Ottoman Empire to come to Palestine in search of work.

The outbreak of World War I in 1914 brought an economic crisis. Palestine was completely cut off and not even mail, and with it donations, got through. Fearing mobilisation by the Turkish army, many fled. Non-Turks were exiled to Tiberias, or worse, to Turkey.

A small group of people, led by Aron Aronson, the agronomist who traced the domestication of wild wheat, and his sister Sarah, formed an espionage unit known as Netzach Israel Lo Yishaker ("the strength of Israel will not lie" I Sam 15:29), abbreviated to NILI. They collected and transmitted information to the British forces in Cairo.

Even prior to the end of the war, France and Britain had divided the Ottoman Empire between them by the Sykes-Picot agreement. Under General Allenby, later Lord of Armageddon (Megiddo), Palestine was conquered by Britain. At the same time, Lord Balfour, in a letter to Lord Rothschild, promised the Jewish people a "national home" in Palestine.

With these events the Ottoman period draws to a close.

Minaret, incorrectly known as David's tower, adjoining the Old City wall.

<table>
<tr><td>Chapter 11</td><td>

British Mandate
1917–1948

</td></tr>
</table>

*F*or some readers, the history of the Holy Land is now part of current events rather than history. The aftermath of the First World War brought changes to Europe and the Middle East. New countries were carved out of the now defunct Ottoman Empire, Iraq and Syria, to name but two.

Jewish volunteers in the allied forces served in the Zion Mule Corps in Gallipoli. Others were part of the Jewish Legion, the 38th, 39th and 40th Battalions of the Royal Fusiliers, in which they wore their own insignia.

The British army followed almost exactly the route taken by Napoleon in 1799. In fact, to quote Lloyd George: "Napoleon's plan was to take Europe from the rear.... This is how the allies won WWI – Palestine then Bulgaria. Constantinople was menaced, Austria threatened from the rear and that caused their army to lose morale".

Grave in the British Military cemetery in Be'er Sheva'.

Middle East after World War I

BLACK SEA

CASPIAN SEA

ITALY

GREECE

TURKEY

MEDITERRANEAN SEA

CRETE

CYPRUS

LEBANON

SYRIA

Damascus

Baghdad

IRAQ

Teheran

IRAN

PALESTINE

JORDAN

Cairo

KUWAIT

PERSIAN GULF

BAHREIN

QATAR

LYBIA

EGYPT

Medina

Mecca

SAUDI ARABIA

DUBAI

MUSCAT+OMAN

RED SEA

SUDAN

YEMEN

Aden

GULF of EDEN

ETHIOPEA

SOMALIA

The capture of the wells of Be'er Sheva' from the Turkish and German armies succeeded, thanks to the courage and perseverance of the ANZACs and the Gurkhas, and opened the way northwards.

The surrender of Jerusalem was a comedy of errors. The Turkish mayor first surrendered to a British mess sergeant and later to the divisional commander. Finally, as befitted the honour of Jerusalem, a formal ceremony was conducted by General Allenby on the steps of the Citadel, just inside the Jaffa Gate.

In 1920, the League of Nations confirmed the French Mandate over Syria and the British Mandate over Mesopotamia as well as the British undertaking to create a national home for the Jews in Palestine. The British appointed Feisal king of the newly created Iraq. Land which had belonged to the Turkish Sultan now became British crown land.

Unrest in the French controlled area of Syria resulted in the attack on Tel Hai and the death of eight defenders, including Joseph Trumpeldor. The

Tel Hai, symbol of the tenacity of the early settlers.

resolution of the Jewish settlers to return to Metulla and Tel Hai meant that the Galilee pan-handle remained part of Palestine and not part of what would eventually be Lebanon.

In 1923, Palestine was divided. The eastern bank of the Jordan was given to Feisal's brother, Abdullah, who was made king of the newly created Kingdom of Jordan. The Jewish national home in Palestine was now limited to the western bank of the Jordan River.

Furthermore, within this area, limitations were placed on the Jews. They could only purchase land along the coastal strip and in the valleys, where the Turks, judging the land to be worthless, had permitted Jewish purchases.

Under the terms of the Mandate the Jewish agency was recognised as the local autonomous body responsible for the economic and social needs of the Palestinian Jews. This covered schools, hospitals, settlements and the control of the Jewish National Fund, which purchased land using money collected from Jews throughout the world.

Many Arabs from the neighbouring areas of Syria and Egypt, and even further afield, continued to come to Palestine, as they had in the Ottoman period, to look for work. Despite setbacks, this was the fastest developing area in the Middle East.

The Palestinian Arabs had the same rights as the Palestinian Jews but were not as well organised. The Moslem community was governed by the Supreme Moslem Council, of whom the Mufti was president until he was deposed by the British. The Arab Executive policy was one of non-cooperation.

The 1920's was a decade of economic stagnation – roads were built and forests planted to provide dole work. A Jewish defence organisation, known as the Hagana, (defence) grew out of the HaShomer (watchman) organisation of the Ottoman period. Mandatory law banned Jews from possessing any weapons, but there was no parallel ban on the Arab population.

The Hagana was unable to offer adequate protection during the widespread Arab riots of 1929 when many Jews were massacred. The surviving Jewish population of Hebron was evacuated by the British.

The Passfield White Paper of 1930 decided that there was to be no further land purchases by Jews and no more Jewish immigration. The reason given for this decision was that a survey had concluded that Palestine was already over-populated and could absorb no more immigrants! World pressure caused these decrees to be abrogated.

Paradoxically, Arab immigration was not curtailed and in fact increased, as demonstrated by Jean Peters in her thesis, later published under the title "From Time Immemorial".

The general Arab uprising of 1936, organised by the Arab Higher Committee, caused the closure of the port of Jaffa. This resulted in the building of a new port in the fast growing Jewish town, Tel Aviv. To combat Arab sabotages on the oil pipeline from Iraq to Haifa, Colonel Orde Wingate was sent to organise Jewish volunteers who would operate under the British army.

Members of these field units would be the forerunners of the Israeli Defence Forces, who will always remember the British colonel who led them with a Bible in his hand, exorting them to take an example from the biblical Israelites, Gideon in particular, and their battles against the numerically superior Canaanites.

During this period over fifty settlements were established on Jewish-owned land in areas where settlement was forbidden. Under Turkish law, the Sultan owned all the land unless he, or his representative, agreed to sell a parcel, which was duly registered (tabu).

Tower and Stockade at Nir David.

The British mandate preserved Ottoman law and the Sultan's land now became Crown land, which the 'crown' could sell if it so desired. The British also preserved the custom that once land had been ploughed the farmer could not be evicted as long as he continued farming, although this did not constitute ownership.

Jewish settlers took advantage of this and overnight a stockade and tower were built and by the time they were detected by the British the land was already ploughed.

In 1939, the first Jew was hanged by the British in the jail in Acco – for being in possession of a pistol.

The refugee internment camp at Atlit.

The rise of the Nazis to power in Germany brought an influx of capital as, on the one hand, the Germans encouraged Jews to leave if they could afford the ransom, and, on the other, the British allowed a limited number of refugees to purchase immigration certificates.

With the outbreak of World War II, Palestinian Jews volunteered for service in the British army but were refused the right to have their own identifying insignia until 1944. Not only were the gates of Palestine closed, but those few vessels reaching the shores with their cargo of refugees were returned to Europe.

Resentment against this policy was kept low-key – the main aim was to defeat the Germans. When it was discovered that the Templars in the German colonies were spying on behalf of the Axis powers, the British rounded them up and shipped them to Australia.

Despite expectations that the end of the war and a change in the British government would alleviate the situation of Holocaust survivors in Europe, this was not to be the case.

The Hagana, and splinter groups, the Irgun (Irgun Zvei Leumi, also known as Etzel) and Lechi (Fighters for the Freedom of Israel, called the Stern Gang by the British) all worked towards breaking the British blockade. Some "illegals" safely reached Palestine, others landed but were caught and interned in camps. The more unfortunate were loaded onto British naval ships and taken to Cyprus. The ship Exodus was returned to Hamburg.

Members of the Irgun and Lechi began to take more active measures against the British forces such as attacks on army bases, trains, police stations and even the CID headquarters in the King David Hotel in Jerusalem.

Reprisals were severe and included curfews and collective punishment against large and innocent sectors of the general public. The frequent use of the gallows came to an end when two British sergeants held, in vain, as hostages to forestall three death sentences from being carried out, were hanged.

"This downward course, which culminated in the relinquishment of the Mandate, could be simply traced by reference, among other things, to each new atrocity in the programme of the Jewish dissident groups". (Cordon & Search Maj. R.D. Wilson p 63).

The British relinquished the Mandate and placed the problem of Palestine in the lap of the United Nations. A committee made up of representatives from eleven neutral countries was sent to Palestine to investigate and suggest a solution.

Under the chairmanship of Jorges Granados of Guatemala, the solution offered by the U.N. Special Committee on Palestine would be known as "The Partition Plan". When the U.N. General Assembly voted on the resolution on 29th November 1947, thirty three countries voted in favour, including the U.S.A., U.S.S.R., and the Commonwealth countries; thirteen voted against, eleven of them Moslem countries; ten abstained, among them Britain.

Evacuation of the 100,000 British troops began almost immediately. Parallel to the evacuation was the increase of Arab attacks on Jewish transport throughout the country. In many instances, settlements and even towns were under siege. Convoys were ambushed and then massacred and looted by Arab mobs from neighbouring villages. The War of Independence had begun.

Remains of charred vehicle at Bab el Wad, on the way to besieged Jerusalem.

The realisation that the Jewish population could not rely on British protection was brought home when seventy eight personnel of the Hadassah Hospital on Mt. Scopus were massacred in full view of British soldiers.

The Jewish population of Jerusalem, 100,000 in number, were under siege and the supplies of severely rationed food and water were down to a week when the first convoys from the coast reached Jerusalem just in time for the Passover festival. But free and safe access to Jerusalem was not yet to be.

With the departure of the last British forces only days away, David Ben Gurion, chairman of the National Council, convened a meeting. On the agenda was the recommendation by U.S.A. Secretary of State Marshall not to establish a state.

"Here you are surrounded by Arabs," he had told the Jewish Agency representative in the U.S.A., indicating the Negev. "Here you are surrounded by other Arabs," he continued, pointing to Galilee. "You have Arab states all around you, and your backs are to the sea. ...The Arabs have regular well-trained armies and heavy arms. How can you hope to hold out?" (O Jerusalem p. 316).

"I dare believe in victory. We shall triumph!" Ben Gurion exhorted the Council members, the majority of whom voted in favour of proclaiming "the birth of a new Jewish nation in the land of Israel".

The High Commissioner was to lower the Union Jack on Friday at midnight. In order not to desecrate the Sabbath, the Declaration of Independence was made at four o'clock in the afternoon.

On the fifth day of the month of Iyar, in the year 5708 of the Hebrew calendar, the 14th May, 1948, the State of Israel was born.

U.N. Palestine Partition Plan 29th November 1947

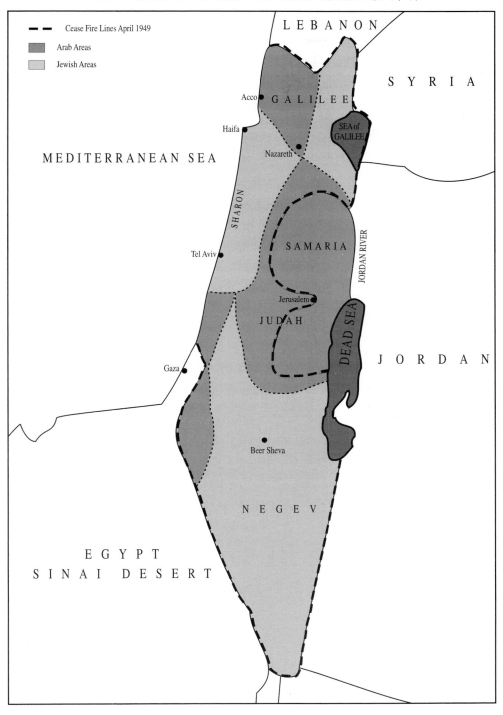

- – – Cease Fire Lines April 1949
- Arab Areas
- Jewish Areas

LEBANON

SYRIA

GALILEE

Acco

Haifa

SEA of GALILEE

MEDITERRANEAN SEA

Nazareth

SHARON

SAMARIA

JORDAN RIVER

Tel Aviv

Jerusalem

JUDAH

DEAD SEA

JORDAN

Gaza

Beer Sheva

NEGEV

EGYPT

SINAI DESERT

Excerpts from the Declaration of Independence:

In the Land of Israel the Jewish people came into being. In this Land was shaped their spiritul, religious and national character ... Here they ... gave to the world the eternal Book of Books ...

In 1897 the First Zionist Congress met at the call of Theodore Herzl ... and gave public voice to the right of the Jewish people to national restoration in their Land ...

This right was acknowledged in the Balfour Declaration on 2 November 1917, and confirmed in the Mandate of the League of Nations, which accorded international validity to the historical connection between the Jewish people and the Land of Israel ...

On 29 November 1947 the General Assembly of the United Nations adopted a resolution calling for the establishment of a Jewish State in the Land of Israel ...

Accordingly we ... proclaim the establishment of the State of Israel ...

It will guarantee freedom of religion and conscience, of language, education and culture. It will safeguard the Holy Places of all religions. It will be loyal to the principles of the United Nations Charter....

Chapter 12	State of Israel

The new state, with no natural resources, without a monetary or postal system, as these had been withdrawn by the British, had barely drawn its first breath when it was bombed by the invading Egyptian army. The armies of Syria, Lebanon, Jordan, Iraq and Saudi Arabia weren't far behind. Other Moslem counties sent additional volunteers and at the same time expelled their Jewish citizens.

With the Soviet Union and the U.S.A. in the lead, various nations recognised the new state. Most were sure that the state and its 650,000 Jewish citizens would not survive.

When reviewing the forty-eight years of Israeli statehood, it appears to be one war after another: the War of Independence (1948-49); the Sinai Campaign (1956); the Six Day War (1967); the War of Attrition (1967-70); the Yom Kippur War (1973-74); Operation Peace for Galilee (Lebanon 1982).

Indeed, Israeli war casualties total over eighteen thousand. Over six thousand, 1% of the 1948 population, in the War of Independence alone.

However, between 1948 and 1995, the country absorbed over 2,500,000 immigrants. In the first two years, almost one and a half million refugees arrived, all of them penniless, most of them without any formal education. Some were remnants of the Holocaust, others had been expelled from Moslem countries. They came from "among the nations, whither they be gone" (Ezekiel 37:21). Yet others came from the free world. The total population of Israel in June 1996 was 5,685,600.

The ma'abarot (transit camps) where the immigrants arriving between 1948 and 1951 were housed in tents, are now towns: Beit Shemesh, Or Akiva, Migdal ha-Emek, Kiryat Shmona, Kiryat Malachi, Eilat, Yerucham, Shlomi and Sderot. In addition, over two hundred agricultural settlements were established.

By the time the next large wave of immigrants arrived in 1955 and 1956, absorption was mainly in new development towns in the underpopulated south. Kiryat Gat, Ofakim, Dimona, Mizpeh Ramon and Netivot were all founded at that time.

The most recent wave was from the former U.S.S.R. (450,000) and from Ethiopia. The transfer of nine thousand Ethiopian Jews, in 1990, using all the planes of El Al, the national airline of Israel, and assisted by the Israeli air force, was seen by television viewers throughout the world.

Mekorot, the Israel water company, completed the national water carrier in 1964 bringing water from Lake Kinneret to the south, thereby fulfilling the biblical prophecy and making the desert bloom once again.

The J.N.F. (Jewish National Fund), which was founded in 1897, has planted over 180 million trees in forests throughout the country. They have developed methods of collecting the maximum amount of rain water and built reservoirs which have brought water sports and recreational fishing to the desert.

New methods of irrigation and farming have been passed on to many Third World countries, some of whom do not, or did not, even recognise the existence of Israel.

Indeed, Israel's achievements are many and varied, but it is the wars which interest historians, so let us look at those wars.

The first stage of the War of Independence lasted from 15th May to 11th June, 1948. During that time there were a number of achievements:

In the south, even though Yad Mordecai fell, the Egyptian advance towards Tel Aviv was halted. In the centre, the Iraqi advance towards Nethania was repulsed. On the Syrian front, Ein Gev fought off an attack but Mishmar ha-Yarden fell, giving the Syrians a foothold on the western side of the Jordan.

In the north, the invasion by Lebanese forces had been prevented but units of the Arab Liberation Army succeeded in penetrating Galilee.

The most crucial battles, though, were probably being fought in the Jerusalem area. The Etzion block, protecting the southern approach to Jerusalem, had fallen and the survivors had been taken prisoner. All attempts to reach the Jewish quarter in the Old City had failed. Over fifty synagogues and most of the quarter would be destroyed by the Jordanians.

Latrun, which controlled the approach to Jerusalem from the coast, was still held by the Arab Legion. The city was down to two days' ration of bread and even water was severely rationed. Fortunately, a rough dirt track had been discovered quite by chance. Nicknamed the "Burma Road", it was at this point passable to human porters only, but soon would be made fit for donkeys and finally vehicles.

The first truce, supervised by the U.N., lasted from 11th June to 9th July. During this time, both sides tried to improve their positions. The only

Latrun, which symbolised the battle for the road to Jerusalem, no-man's-land until 1967, is now a memorial to the fallen of the Armoured Corps.

agreement secured was the demilitarization of Mt. Scopus, where the Hadassah Hospital and Hebrew University were.

During the next ten days fighting, the Israelis had a number of successes. Part of the Arab population of Lydda and Ramleh were expelled, part fled, but many remained and became Israeli citizens. The vital springs at Rosh ha-Ayin were captured and pumping water to Jerusalem resumed. The Syrians were not dislodged from their bridgehead, but failed to overrun Kibbutz Ayelet ha-Shachar.

Nazareth surrendered and, after it, all the Arab positions in Lower Galilee. Most of the Arab population remained and they too became citizens of Israel. Latrun was still in Jordanian hands but the "Burma Road" was in full use and the railway line connecting Jerusalem to the coast was firmly in Israeli hands, ensuring free access to Jerusalem.

The second truce began on 18th July but was breached almost immediately. The Latrun pumping station, under U.N. control, was destroyed by the Arab Legion. A hastily-laid pipeline along the "Burma Road" kept Jerusalem provided with water.

The terms of the truce, rejected by both sides, included making "free ports" of Haifa and Lydda Airport (both held by Israel) and granting Jerusalem and the Negev to the Arabs.

A major effort was now made by the Israeli forces to open the road to the Negev and to clear it of Egyptian troops. The next step was the capture of Be'er Sheva' and from there, southwards to Um Rash Rash (modern Eilat), thereby ensuring Israel's access to the Red Sea.

Some Arabs fled as the Israeli army advanced. When hostilities ended, many chose not to live under Israeli rule and refused the opportunity to return. Those who remained make up 17% of the population of Israel today. As citizens of Israel, they vote in Israeli elections and are represented in the Knesset, Israel's Parliament. They are exempt from service in the Israeli Defence Force.

Armistice agreements were signed with Egypt on 24th February, 1949, with Jordan on 4th March, with Lebanon on 23rd March, and finally, with Syria on 20th July, 1949. These agreements were meant "to facilitate the transition from truce to permanent peace". In actuality, until 1967, the demarcation lines became the de facto borders, despite violations.

The Gaza strip came under Egyptian occupation and the Hashemite Kingdom of Jordan annexed those parts of Palestine not included in the State of Israel, generally known as the West Bank. Palestine ceased to exist.

During the ensuing eight years there were at least six thousand infiltrations into Israel, over four hundred Israelis were killed and nine hundred injured. Contrary to the terms of the agreements, the U.N. was not able to assure Israel's access to Jerusalem via Latrun or to the university and hospital on Mt. Scopus.

In 1955, Egypt and Syria, who had signed a military pact, began receiving massive arms supplies from the Soviet bloc. Although the U.S., Britain and France continued to equip the Arab armies, Israel had succeeded in persuading France alone to sell her arms.

Syria attacked Israeli fishing boats on the Kinneret. Terrorist infiltrations from Jordan and Egypt made life in the southern parts of Israel perilous. The Red Sea was closed to Israeli shipping to Eilat. (The Suez canal had never been open to Israeli vessels).

Israeli fears of a joint Arab attack coincided with British and French apprehension over the threat posed by Egyptian control over the newly nationalised Suez canal. The Anglo-French plan to invade Egypt included an Israeli invasion of the Sinai peninsula.

Between 29th October and 5th November, 1956, in what would be known as the Sinai campaign, Israel conquered the Gaza strip and the entire Sinai peninsula, stopping ten miles from the canal. Egypt's military infrastructure in Sinai was severely damaged, the Gulf of Eilat was reopened and the terrorist bases were destroyed.

Due to heavy U.S. pressure, the Anglo-French invasion of Egypt accomplished nothing. U.S. threats to expel Israel from the U.N. and to impose economic sanctions, together with an undertaking by the U.N. and all the major maritime powers, guaranteeing freedom of navigation for Israel, both in the canal and in the gulf, and U.N. control of the Gaza strip, base for terrorist attacks on Israel, secured a complete Israeli withdrawal from Sinai.

Within days the undertakings were shown to be worthless. The canal was never opened to Israeli shipping and the Egyptians replaced the U.N. administration of the Gaza strip.

Egypt and Syria united to form the United Arab Republic and their attempts to "lead" the Arab world resulted in U.S. intervention in the civil war in Lebanon and Anglo-U.S. support to keep secure Jordan's throne for King Hussein, with the agreement of Israel, who permitted use of her airspace.

After a few years of relative quiet, terrorist infiltrations were once more on the increase, penetrating to the heart of the country. Syrian positions bombarded Israel's northern settlements. President Nasser of Egypt unilaterally ordered U.N. troops to leave Sinai, where they had been stationed since 1957, and moved his army in.

Once more the Straits of Tiran were closed to Israeli shipping. Pacts were signed between Egypt and Jordan, Iraq, Kuwait and Algeria and the Arab world prepared for war against Israel. "In five days we shall liquidate the State of Israel" was the official forecast of the Egyptian army. "Four days", was the Syrian prophecy.

According to international law, war had been declared on Israel. Anticipating her impending destruction, the impotent world looked on. Only France acted – by decreeing an arms embargo on Israel.

It was clear that Israel had only herself to rely on and so, on the 5th June, 1967, a preemptive air strike was launched. Within hours, over four hundred Egyptian planes were destroyed. Within four days the Israeli forces had taken the entire Sinai peninsula and were on the banks of the Suez canal.

Explaining why he agreed to a ceasefire Nasser said: "We had no defences on the west side of the canal. Not a single soldier stood between the enemy and the capital."

Intermediaries, including U.N. mediator General Odd Bull, advised King Hussein that Israel had no intention of attacking Jordan. Deceived by Egypt into thinking that her army had the upper hand, Jordan opened fire along the entire border, shelling even Tel Aviv. The main brunt of the attack was, of course, Jerusalem.

Israel, June 1967

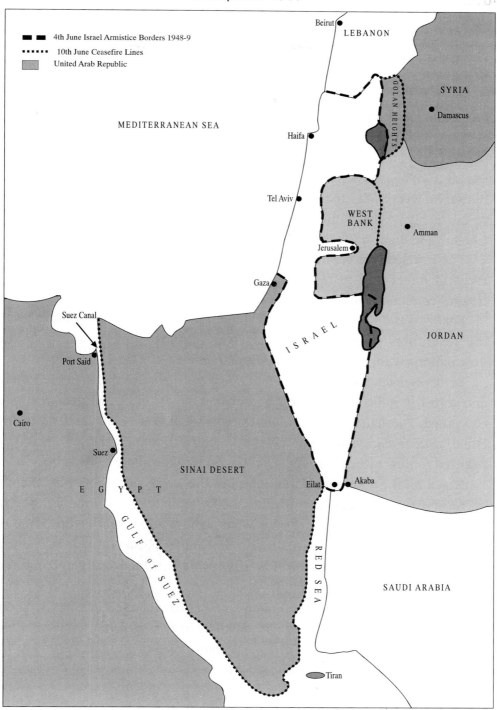

4th June Israel Armistice Borders 1948-9
10th June Ceasefire Lines
United Arab Republic

LEBANON

Beirut

SYRIA

Damascus

MEDITERRANEAN SEA

Haifa

GOLAN HEIGHTS

Tel Aviv

WEST
BANK

Amman

Jerusalem

ISRAEL

JORDAN

Gaza

Suez Canal

Port Said

Cairo

Suez

SINAI DESERT

E G Y P T

GULF of SUEZ

Eilat Akaba

RED SEA

SAUDI ARABIA

Tiran

Within three days, the Israeli army was on the banks of the Jordan River. The capture of the old city of Jerusalem resulted in large Israeli casualties because of the desire not to inflict any damage on the Holy sites. Jews had free access to the Temple Mount – for the first time since the Romans destroyed the Temple in the year 70.

Due to the strategic and topographic advantage of the Syrian positions and the ineffectiveness of Israeli bombing, the Israeli forces had not advanced in the north. When Syria rejected the ceasefire agreed upon by Egypt and Jordan, the decision was taken to advance, despite the knowledge that the Israeli losses would be high. Within thirty hours the Israeli army had taken the entire Golan Heights and was on the main road leading to Damascus.

The Israelis were euphoric. Surely Jordan, and possibly Egypt, would join Israel in direct face to face talks which would lead to fully-fledged peace treaties combined with an Israeli withdrawal.

Reality was different. At the Arab summit in Khartoum in September 1967, the resolution passed unanimously was: "No recognition of Israel, no negotiations with Israel, no peace with Israel".

Settlements in the Jordan and Beit Shean valleys were shelled from Jordan and terrorist infiltrations posed a constant threat and a cycle of reprisals continued. Through it all the bridges connecting the West Bank, and, indirectly Israel, with Jordan, and ultimately the Arab world, remained open. Terrorism resorted to new tactics – the hijacking of an El Al airplane to Algeria.

Based on the assumption that, because the Israeli army consisted mainly of reservists, the economy would not be able to withstand long-term mobilisation, the Egyptians began what would be known as the "War of Attrition". The main aim was to lower morale within Israel by daily casualties. Israeli retaliation was deep within Egypt and included bringing captured Russian radar equipment back intact.

Russian crews manned newly installed SAM 2 and SAM 3 missiles and flew Soviet aircraft, four of them brought down by Israeli Air Force planes. Fearing a confrontation with Russia, Secretary of State Rogers pressured Israel to set aside her demand for direct negotiations.

U.N. Ambassador Jarring brokered a ceasefire between Israel and Egypt and Jordan, as a preview to direct talks. Within days, and in direct contravention of the terms of the agreement, Russia installed anti-aircraft missiles along the entire eastern front. The seeds for the 1973 war had been sown.

In September 1970, henceforth to be known as "Black September", King Hussein expelled all the terrorist organisations from Jordan. Fatah claimed that over twenty thousand casualties had been inflicted.

Syrian forces invaded Jordan but retreated when Israel openly moved her armour to the Syrian border and, with the U.S., Israel advised both Syria and Russia that any interference in Jordan would have severe consequences.

The terrorist organisations had not yet gained a foothold in Lebanon and most of their activities were directed against Israeli and Jewish targets throughout the world. Over the next three years the borders were reasonably quiet, but this was merely the lull before the storm.

The storm broke on 6th October, 1973, on the afternoon of Yom Kippur (the Day of Atonement). Blinded by the conviction that Egypt was not ready for another war and that Syria would not go to war without Egypt, Israel was taken completely unawares.

In the south, the Egyptian forces crossed the canal to be faced by about six hundred unprepared reservists, many of them in the middle of praying. Two hundred kilometres (125 miles) separated the canal from Israel.

Within hours the Egyptian forces had prepared ten bridges and fifty ferries and were streaming into Sinai, under an umbrella of Russian missiles against which the Israel Air Force was virtually defenceless. After a week of fighting, their maximum penetration was ten kilometres (6 miles) along the length of the canal.

In the north, waves of Syrian forces swept onto the Golan, twenty-five kilometres (15 miles) east to west at its widest point. They advanced towards the Kinneret, protected by the same Russian umbrella.

In forty-eight hours they reached their maximum penetration – five kilometres from the Bnot Yaacov bridge over the Jordan River. On 8th October, the Israeli counter-attack began and by the 10th the Israeli forces had reached the former ceasefire lines. Damascus was forty kilometres away.

Israeli appeals to the U.S., her only supplier for replacements to her depleted armoury, were answered by evasion – President Nixon and Secretary of State Kissinger wanted a "limited Israeli defeat". The Russian airlift continued unabated.

Kissinger tried to negotiate a ceasefire in situ by which the Egyptians would be in control of the entire canal. When Sadat refused, the U.S. decided to begin its airlift. Europe united in its refusal to allow American planes refueling rights, thereby causing an added delay. Eventually the planes were permitted to refuel at the American-leased base in the Azores.

The tide on the Egyptian front began to turn on 15th October when Israeli units crossed the canal westwards. Only on the 21st did Egypt acknowledge

The Knesset, Israeli House of Parliament.

this presence, but by then the Egyptian Third Army was under siege and Cairo was threatened. The U.S. and Russia sponsored a ceasefire resolution which went into effect on the 22nd.

Sporadic fighting continued as the Egyptian forces tried to improve their positions, to no avail. Israel allowed medical supplies through to the beseiged third army.

On the 27th, fighting finally ended. Israel lost over 2,500 soldiers. With a population of two and a half million, this was a ratio of one to a thousand. An agreement was signed on 18th January, 1974.

On the Syrian front, fighting continued until a similar agreement was signed on 31st May, 1974. A law, passed by the Knesset in 1981, annexed the Golan Heights, making them an integral part of the State of Israel. Israeli citizenship was offered to the Druze villagers, none of whom had left in the wars of 1967 or 1973.

In 1977, very faint winds of change began to blow – President Sadat visited Israel and addressed the Knesset. At Camp David, on 26th March, 1979, the first peace between Israel and one of her neighbours was signed by Menachem Begin and Anwar Sadat.

For the first time since 1948, the front-line now moved to the border with Lebanon. Southern Lebanon had been completely taken over by the various Palestinian terrorist groups. Almost daily, or nightly, Katyusha rockets were fired into Israeli towns and settlements, from Naharia in the west to Metulla and Kiryat Shmona in the east.

On 5th June, 1982 Israeli troops, welcomed by Lebanese villagers, crossed the border to set in motion the Peace for Galilee campaign. Expulsion of all the terrorists was only partially achieved. An agreement was signed between Israel and Lebanon on 17th May, 1983.

Israel's withdrawal was not complete and at present (1996) Israel patrols a fourteen-kilometre strip together with the South Lebanese Army, which is trained and financed by Israel.

1994 and 1995 have been momentous years. First was the breakthough with the Palestinian groups followed by the peace treaty with Jordan.

From here on **YOU** are a witness to the events. I hope that you will follow them with greater interest and understanding, now that you have a deeper knowledge of this tiny, but turbulent, corner of the world.

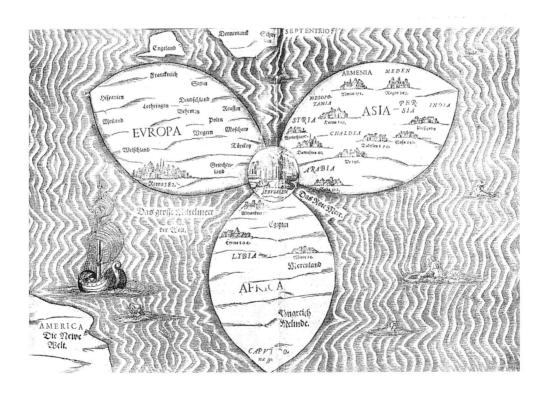

The Land of Israel, where three continents meet, and Jerusalem in the centre, as depicted in a schematic map of the Middle Ages.

Bibliography

The bibliography does not list every source used in writing this book. Hebrew references have been omitted as have academic publications. Each book listed has its own bibliography for those really bitten by the history bug.

Use the bibliography as a stepping-stone along the historical path in which you are most interested. Browse in your local library and bookshop. For those whose "appetites" have merely been "whetted", a representative selection of novels has been included.

Ben-Sasson, Editor, *A History of the Jewish People*, Weidenfeld & Nicolson, U.K., 1976.

Benvenisti M., *The Crusaders in the Holy Land*, MacMillan, N.Y., 1970.

Canaan Tewfik, *Mohammedan Saints and Sanctuaries in Palestine*, (1927), Ariel, Israel, 1990.

Collins & Lapierre, *O Jerusalem*, Simon & Schuster, Inc., N.Y., 1972.

Comay J., *The World's Greatest Story*, Weidenfeld & Nicolson, London, 1978.

Cornfeld G. Freedman D.N., *Archaeology of the Bible Book by Book*, A. & C. Black Ltd., London, 1977.

Cornfeld G., *Josephus - The Jewish War*, Masada Press, Israel, 1982.

Danby H., *The Mishnah*, Oxford University Press.

Dimont M.I., *Jews, God and History*, Simon & Schuster, Inc., N.Y., 1962.

Greenfield Murray S., The Jews' Secret Fleet, Gefen Publishing House, Jerusalem, Israel, 1987.

Hitti P., *History of Syria*, MacMillan, N.Y., 1951.

Holmes R.H., *The Fore-Runners*, Herald, Missouri, 1981.

Idinopulos T.A., *Jerusalem Blessed, Jerusalem Cursed*, Ivan R. Dee, U.S.A., 1991.

Josephus Flavius, *The Complete Works of Josephus*, Kregel Publications, Michigan, 1960/1995.

Kaufman Y., *The Religion of Israel*, Schoken Books, N.Y., 1972.

Kobler F., *Napoleon and the Jews*, Schoken, N.Y., 1976.

Kushner D., Editor, *Palestine in the Late Ottoman Period*, Israel, 1986.

Le Strange G., *Palestine Under the Moslem*, Houghton, Boston, 1890, Ariel, Israel, 1990.

Lorch N., *One Long War*, Keter, Israel, 1976.

Maccoby H., Editor, *Judaism on Trial*, Littman, Washington, 1993.

Martin R.C., *Islam*, Prentice-Hall, N.J., 1982.

Payne R., *The Dream and the Tomb*, Dorset Press, N.Y., 1984.

Peters J., *From Time Immemorial*, Michael Joseph, London, 1985.

Pickthall M.M., *The Meaning of the Glorious Koran*, Albany University, N.Y., 1976.

Pixner B., *With Jesus Through the Galilee*, Corazin, 1992.

Rowley H.H., *The Growth of the Old Testament*, Torch Books, N.Y., 1963.

Schiffman L.H., *Reclaiming the Dead Sea Scrolls*, Jewish Publication Society, Philadelphia, 1994.

Scholem G., *Kabbalah*, Keter, Jerusalem, 1988.

Schroeder G.L., *Genesis and the Big Bang*, Bantam Books, U.K., 1990.

Schur N., *Christian Pilgrimage to the Holy Land*, Dvir, Israel, 1992.

Soncino, *Books of the Bible*, Soncino Press, London.

Spafford Verster B., *Our Jerusalem*, American Colony, Jerusalem, 1950/1980.

Spirydon S.N., *Annals of Palestine 1821-1841* – Monk Neophitis, (1928), Ariel, Israel, 1990.

Steinsaltz A., *The Essential Talmud*, Bantam Books, U.S., 1976.

Sykes C., *Crossroads to Israel: Palestine from Balfour to Bevin*, London, 1965.

Twain Mark, *Innocents Abroad*, 1868.

Van der Kam J.C., *The Dead Sea Scrolls Today*, Wm. B. Eerdmans, Michigan, 1994.

Wilson R.D., *Cordon and Search*, Aldershot, U.K., 1949.

Yadin Y., *Bar Kochba*, Weidenfeld & Nicolson, London.

Yadin Y., *Hatzor*, Weidenfeld & Nicolson, London.

Yadin Y., *Masada*, Weidenfeld & Nicolson, London.

Yadin Y., *The Temple Scroll*, Weidenfeld & Nicolson, London.

The New Encyclopedia of Archaeological Excavations in the Holy Land, Israel Exploration Society and Carta, 1993.

The New Testament, Various Editions.

Journals:

Biblical Archaeology.

Biblical Archaeology Review.

Novels:

Auel J., *The Clan of the Cave Bear*.

Michener J., *The Source*.

Steinberg M., *As a Driven Leaf*.

Uris L., *Exodus*.

Uris L., *The Haj*.

Wouk H., *The Hope*.

General Index

The index includes people, places and subjects.

* –　places appearing on the general map on page 9 followed by their reference
　　number on that map.

\# –　places appearing on other maps or in photographs followed by the relevant
　　page number.

List of Maps